SECRETS OF PRODUCTIVE PEOPLE

50 Techniques to Get Things Done

Mark Forster

To Lucy, the most productive person I know.

SECRETS OF PRODUCTIVE PEOPLE

50 Techniques to Get Things Done

Mark Forster

First published in Great Britain in 2015 by John Murray Learning

British Library Cataloguing in Publication Data: a catalogue record for this title is available from the British Library.

ISBN 9781473608856

eISBN 9781473608863

1

Typeset by Cenveo® Publisher Services.

Printed and bound in Great Britain by CPI Group (UK) Ltd., Croydon, CR0 4YY.

John Murray Learning policy is to use papers that are natural, renewable and recyclable products and made from wood grown in sustainable forests. The logging and manufacturing processes are expected to conform to the environmental regulations of the country of origin.

Carmelite House
50 Victoria Embankment
London EC4Y 0DZ
www.hodder.co.uk

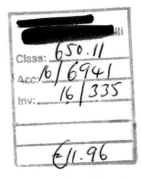

CONTENTS

INTRODUCTION

Productivity is one of those ill-defined words which are often heard in a management context. The general image of a 'productive person' is of someone rather docile who slavishly processes the work given to them and comes up with a satisfactory result – satisfactory that is to the managers who gave them the task. The person is productive in the way a factory hen is productive. It's one step down from being called 'efficient' – the people who manage the chicken factory are 'efficient', not the hens.

So productivity has the rather negative image of rows of people churning out large quantities of work without much imaginative input into the nature of that work.

The image changes though when we put the concept of productivity into a different context. Pause for a moment and ask yourself, 'Who are the truly productive figures in the course of human history?' Try and write down off the top of your head a short list of three to five people.

Do that now, before you continue reading.

You will almost certainly find that the historical figures on your short list were most definitely not rather docile people who slavishly processed the work given to them. If you've done the exercise properly they will be people who have made a real and measurable difference to the world, usually for the better. They will be people of great achievements and who have made the world gasp in amazement. One of their great qualities will be that of originality.

My own short list includes three figures about whom I will talk in more detail in Chapter 2. These are Isaac Newton, Vincent van Gogh and Henry Ford. You probably cannot imagine yourself in your wildest dreams being productive in the way that these three were productive. And you are probably right – you are never going to equal their achievements in their own fields. But how about in your own field? Can you apply the principles that they used, consciously or unconsciously, to your own work, your own lifetime passion, or even to your leisure time, so that you produce results which are every bit as amazing to you yourself, your colleagues, your customers, clients, friends and family as my examples' results were to the world at large?

Surprisingly the answer is almost certainly 'Yes, you can'.

As Louann Brizendine, author of *The Female Brain and The Male Brain* says in a review of David Shenk's *The Genius In All of Us*, 'The notion that relentless, deliberate practice changes the brain and thus our abilities has been undervalued over the past 30 years in favour of the concept of "innate giftedness".'

Relentless and deliberate practice? Changing the brain in order to change our abilities? Yes, that is precisely what lies at the basis of the sort of productivity that Newton, Van Gogh and Ford exhibited. What they did in short was to grow their brains to fit their area of productivity. You can do exactly the same. This book will show you how.

HOW TO USE THIS BOOK

Here's one difference between a productive person and other people. Faced with the ideas in a book like this many people's attitude is 'This wouldn't work for me because...' and then they stop any further consideration.

The productive person on the other hand has the attitude 'How can I use this?' He or she is always looking for ideas that will make a difference. If you are one of these people then make the ideas in this book your own, change them to fit your own needs, possibly even use them in totally different ways from what I have envisaged.

Some of you will prefer to read the book from cover to cover. If you do this you will find that it follows a logical progression in which later chapters build on earlier chapters. I suggest that you read the book fairly quickly and then go back and try out the suggestions that struck you as particularly interesting or useful.

On the other hand some of you will want to dip into the book and read those chapters that particularly appeal to you. This works fine too because each chapter either can stand on its own or references you back to any previous chapters that are necessary to understand it.

Whichever method you use there are two essential chapters that I recommend everyone to read and try out. These are Chapter 6 (How to get great ideas) and Chapter 9 (Productive time management). These two together form the basis for changing your brain to become truly productive.

THE BASICS OF PRODUCTIVITY

What exactly is productivity? Is it just getting a lot of stuff done, or is there more to it than that? This part of the book looks in detail at the two most important components of productivity and shows you how you too can join the ranks of truly productive people.

1 WHAT IS PRODUCTIVITY?

*Confront the difficult while it is still easy; accomplish the great
task by a series of small acts.*
Tao te Ching

*Amateurs sit and wait for inspiration, the rest of us just get up
and go to work.*
Stephen King

*Productivity is never an accident. It is always the result
of a commitment to excellence, intelligent planning,
and focused effort.*
Paul J. Meyer

*Work is a process, and any process needs to be controlled. To
make work productive, therefore, requires building the
appropriate controls into the process of work.*
Peter F. Drucker

*The routines of almost all famous writers, from Charles
Darwin to John Grisham, similarly emphasize specific starting
times, or number of hours worked, or words written. Such
rituals provide a structure to work in, whether or not the
feeling of motivation or inspiration happens to be present.*
Oliver Burkeman

Often when productivity is discussed it sounds as if it is just
about getting stuff done. It sometimes seems as if it's a synonym
for 'efficient'. Indeed there is no doubt about the fact that a
highly productive person must be efficient. If the basic routines of
one's work are not under control then it is very difficult to work
at the highest level of genuine productivity. Yet productivity goes
a long way beyond mere efficiency. It is much more a matter of
creativity. The truly productive person is intensely creative.

Unfortunately we all know people who claim to be 'creative people' who are anything but productive. They wait around for inspiration to strike and on the rare occasions when it does they set off in a blaze of enthusiasm. Sometimes they produce good work before the enthusiasm dies, more often they don't and the new project withers from lack of attention.

This is the exact opposite of Isaac Newton, Vincent van Gogh and Henry Ford, the three intensely productive people I mentioned in the introduction. Did they wait around for inspiration to strike? No, they got their inspiration by working consistently on their projects. Did they set off in a blaze of enthusiasm which quickly died down? No, they worked consistently and methodically on the project until it was completed.

There are of course many aspects to productivity. But I want to highlight the two elements that seem most essential to me: Creativity and Efficiency.

You can make a formula of them: Productivity = Creativity × Efficiency.

The advantage of looking at it like this is that you can see clearly that if either creativity or efficiency drops to zero then so does productivity. However creative you are, you cannot be productive without some degree of efficiency. Conversely however efficient you are you cannot be productive without some degree of creativity.

Looking at the formula, you see that you can improve your productivity by improving either your creativity or your efficiency. For many people who already consider themselves very creative, there may be more scope for raising their productivity by improving their efficiency than by trying to raise their creativity yet further.

This book will talk about both creativity and efficiency in detail and how they are both linked, but in the meantime here are three action points for you to consider:

1 CREATIVITY COMES MAINLY FROM QUESTIONING THE PROBLEM

The most important aspect of creativity is to keep questioning the situation. The creative person gets their motive power not so much from goals as from questions. Uncreative people set themselves goals like 'Raise sales by 5 per cent this quarter' and then make a plan and try to carry it out rigidly. Unfortunately plans have a habit of coming unstuck with the result that action stalls.

A creative person will ask questions, such as 'How can we raise sales by 5 per cent this quarter?' or even better 'Why are our sales not rising as fast as we hoped?' The second question in particular may lead to a whole series of further questions and investigations. This is not something which should only be done at the planning stage, but is a continuing dynamic process.

This questioning of the situation goes on for as long as there is a situation to question. Sir Isaac Newton kept a running list of *quaestiones* (Latin for 'questions') which formed the basis of his experiments.

Try this little experiment. Select a situation in your work or personal life which you would like to improve. Now write out a list of questions you could ask about this situation. Don't try to answer the questions at this stage; just list them. Once you have got between ten and twelve questions, put the list away for a few hours. Then come back to it and see if you can add any more questions. Don't worry if you can't think of any more, but many people find that they can come up with some very good additional questions after taking a short break from thinking about them.

2 EFFICIENCY COMES MAINLY FROM GOOD PROCESSES CONSISTENTLY APPLIED

It may seem strange to you that producing creative solutions is more about having effective processes than about anything else. But if you look at the five quotations at the beginning of this chapter you can see that this is exactly what the authors were talking about.

Consider this. Having asked yourself the questions in the previous exercise, how are you going to answer them? Some of them may require a good deal of research, experimentation or discussion. All of them will require persistent and methodical action to put your findings into effect.

The heart of efficiency is systems and processes. These come in a sort of hierarchy. At the bottom level are all the everyday routine processes which form the backdrop of your daily life. Going to bed, getting up, exercise, eating, email, reading, travel to and from work, tidying and so on.

In order to be productive, you must have these low-level processes completely under control. If any of these are not working properly, they will have a major negative impact on your productivity. Every bit of time you have to spend unnecessarily sorting out these routines is time you could be spending on real productive work.

Above the low-level processes there will be higher-level processes specific to a particular project or group of projects. Again it is of the utmost importance to get these processes working smoothly so that you don't have to spend unnecessary time on them. For example in the context of a small business, there is little point in having grand plans for expansion if your processes for dealing with new customers, following up existing customers and getting paid for work done are incapable of coping even with your existing volume of work. Systems like these need to be worked out carefully in advance – before they are needed.

As an exercise, have a look at the simple daily routines of your life and identify one which is not working as well for you as it should. Invest some time sorting it out so that it will no longer be a problem. You know it's not a problem when it's working so well that you don't have to think about it anymore. Once you have succeeded in doing that with one routine, see if there are any others which need some sorting out.

3 PRODUCTIVITY IS A PERSISTENT AND CONSISTENT INTERACTION BETWEEN CREATIVITY AND EFFICIENCY

One definition of productivity would be 'creative ideas brought into existence'. To bring your creative ideas into actual existence requires one more ingredient – persistence. Included in persistence is the factor of consistency. One of the reasons that persistence and consistency tend to be undervalued, is that their results tend to look easy.

If we think of the dazzling display that a virtuoso violinist produces, we are just seeing the public face of countless practice sessions carried out hour after hour every day with scarcely an exception. There's a story about a society woman who gushed to the great pianist Horowitz after a performance 'I'd give anything to be able to play like you'. To which his reply was simply 'No, you wouldn't'.

To bring oneself up to world class in any given subject is reputed to require around 10,000 hours of focused work. Allowing for a few inevitable and unavoidable breaks, that represents an average of three hours a day every day for ten years spent solely on practice. All the other demands of life have of course to be fitted round that.

The figure of 10,000 hours is to obtain the very highest standard. Fortunately for the rest of us a lower standard may be perfectly adequate for our purposes, and that would require a lesser number of hours. It's amazing what progress can be made in even as little as forty hours, provided it is consistent and focused. It may well be that you have no desire to reach world standard in any subject, but whatever standard you do aspire to will require the appropriate number of hours.

You have to put in the hours. And to put in the hours means that you are not allowing anything else to take away from those hours. That's why it is so important not to be wasting time over the low-level routines of your life because they are not running properly. Putting in the hours also means that you don't take on more projects than you have time for. If you over-schedule yourself the result will be that *all* your projects fail to be up to the standard they should be.

As an exercise, pick one on-going project that you would like to have in your life but don't at the moment. For this particular exercise it's best to use a personal project rather than a work one. Something like learning a language or a musical instrument, getting fit or training for a particular sport would be ideal. Bearing in mind the standard you would like to achieve, decide how many hours of practice in total you think you would need to reach that standard. Then work out how many hours a day for how long it would take to reach that number of hours. Juggle with the figures until you reach something you believe you actually might be able do if you decided to. Next question: What would it take to rearrange your life so you really could do it?

That's as far as this exercise goes. You don't have to put your plan into effect (unless you want to of course). The point of the exercise is to show how important it is to make a realistic assessment of what is involved when you take on a new project or decide to take an existing one really seriously.

Putting it all together

We have seen that productivity is essentially a matter of bringing our creative ideas into fruition. Without creativity productivity is reduced to mere efficiency. Without bringing our creative ideas to fruition they remain just ideas, mere pipe dreams.

The key that brings our creative ideas into fruition is consistent action. This demands a hierarchy of good systems, both to keep the normal requirements of daily life from interfering and to provide the processes by which our ideas are turned into reality.

The essential requirement is time. Success in any project is usually dependent on the number of hours worked on it per day. We must therefore ensure that the time available for a major project is not encroached upon by unnecessary or inefficient routine work processes, or by competing projects.

In this book we will look more closely at all these aspects of productivity – most especially the creative process itself and how we can ensure that the necessary consistent work is done to bring our ideas to fruition.

In the next chapter we will be looking at three very different people from history whose productivity both amazed the world and changed it forever. What lessons can we learn from them?

2 LEARN FROM HISTORY

Excellence is an art won by training and habituation. We do not act rightly because we have virtue or excellence, but we rather have those because we have acted rightly. We are what we repeatedly do. Excellence, then, is not an act but a habit.
Aristotle

Augustus expressed his surprise that Alexander did not regard it as a greater task to set in order the empire which he had won than to win it.
Plutarch

It had long since come to my attention that people of accomplishment rarely sat back and let things happen to them. They went out and happened to things.
Leonardo da Vinci

Ordinary people think merely of spending time, great people think of using it.
Arthur Schopenhauer

Productivity is being able to do things that you were never able to do before.
Franz Kafka

I'd like to give you three examples of people from history who are generally recognized as having been extremely productive. I have chosen historical figures rather than contemporary ones because it is easier to get an overall picture of their achievements over a lifetime. Using historical figures has the disadvantage that that they are all male – many women in historical times were highly productive but their achievements were often denigrated and not recorded in detail.

I've chosen Western figures for the simple reason that the culture in which they operated will be more comprehensible to the majority of readers of this book. Nevertheless there were many prodigies of productivity in non-Western cultures, such as Avicenna, whose writings were the basis of medical knowledge in both West and East for over half a millennium, or Shen Kuo, the inventor of the magnetic compass centuries before its use was known in the West.

1 SIR ISAAC NEWTON (1642–1727) – QUESTIONING THE UNIVERSE

'If I have ever made any valuable discoveries, it has been due more to patient attention, than to any other talent'.
Isaac Newton

Sir Isaac Newton is one of the towering figures of science. His scientific discoveries are still the underpinning of most of our modern understanding of the world, and few other people have made so great a contribution to the development of today's society.

Yet he did not even start to learn mathematics until he reached university at the age of 19. There his academic performance was undistinguished, though he was deeply involved in his own private studies. Among other achievements during his life, he discovered gravitational force and established the three Universal Laws of Motion, the Binomial Theorem and the calculus, invented the reflecting telescope, investigated the nature of light and wrote the *Principia Mathematica* a book which provided the mathematical tools for the scientific revolution.

In between times he sat in Parliament, was Master of the Mint and President of the Royal Society.

What is the main lesson that we can learn from Newton about how to be productive? He seems to be so far above us in terms of achievement that how he worked would appear almost irrelevant to us. Yet I think we can learn a lot from him. In the above quote he gives 'patient attention' as his chief talent. Patient attention to what? I believe the root of his patient attention was to finding the answers to the questions he was asking. I've already mentioned in Chapter 1 how he used to keep a list of questions. This is something we can all imitate to good effect even at the level of our everyday lives and work.

If you've not done the exercise in section 1 of Chapter 1, then you might like to try it now. If you have, then you can extend it by taking one of the questions you thought of and writing out between three and five possible answers to it. Some of your answers may be actions you could take; others might be investigations you could make. Put the list away for a few hours and then see if you can add any more answers to the list. Then pick the best answer and take some action on it.

2 VINCENT VAN GOGH (1853–1890) – REGULAR FOCUSED ATTENTION

'Great things are done by a series of small things brought together.'
Vincent van Gogh

Today Van Gogh is one of the most popular painters who has ever existed, and his works sell by the million in reproduction. This is exactly what he would have wanted – his vision was to create a new form of art which was accessible to ordinary people in a way in which most of the paintings of his time weren't.

The amazing thing about Van Gogh is that he was almost completely self-taught, not starting to paint until his late 20s. And something just as amazing is that he described his artistic progress in detailed letters to his brother Theo, letters which fill several thick volumes in the standard edition. So not only is he one of the greatest Dutch painters, he is also one of the great writers in the Dutch language (and French too – a third of his letters are in French).

What lesson can we learn from Van Gogh? In little over a decade he produced a huge body of work: 860 oil paintings and 1,300 watercolours, drawings, sketches and prints. During this time he was always experimenting, always seeking to improve the way that he could portray the essence of his subjects.

His work was the cumulative result of sufficient, regular, focused attention. In my book *Get Everything Done and Still Have Time to Play* I call this the key to success. How much is sufficient? How regular is regular, and how focused does attention need to be?

We have the figures for Van Gogh, so let's work it out: 860 oil paintings over a decade is an average of 86 a year. That's one oil painting every 4¼ days. Plus five other pieces of artwork every two weeks!

That's what it takes to be Vincent van Gogh. No, he didn't just sit around until inspiration struck and then produce a picture of some sunflowers, then sit around a bit more until he felt like painting a drawbridge over a canal and so on.

What results would you get if you put this sort of regular, focused attention into *your* favourite project?

3 HENRY FORD (1863–1947) – THE ANSWER IS A BETTER SYSTEM

'There is no man living who isn't capable of doing more than he thinks he can do.'
Henry Ford

Henry Ford left his family farm at the age of 16 to work as an apprentice machinist. He then supported himself and his family by farming and running a sawmill, until at the age of 28 he became an engineer with the Edison Illuminating Company. From then on he hardly looked back, becoming one of the richest and best known people in the world. He is famous for the mass production of inexpensive goods, such as the Model T Ford automobile, coupled with high wages for workers. He also introduced an innovative franchise system for dealerships which made his products available at the local level, first in the United States and around the world.

More than anything else, the focus of Ford's work was on systems. By developing the right systems, whether they were the assembly line or the franchise network or any one of numerous others, he revolutionized business practices, putting the expensive automobile within the reach of the ordinary wage-earner.

Virtually any recurring problem can be solved by working out a system to deal with it. So what were some of the problems that Henry Ford solved?

- More than twenty years after the invention of the automobile, it remained an exotic vehicle only the well-off could afford to buy.
- Because of this there were no local dealerships for the mass market and consequently little competition or incentive to cut prices.
- The low wages paid to workers in the automobile industry resulted in high staff turnover and loss of trained personnel.

As we have seen, once a problem has been identified you can start asking questions about it.

As an exercise, identify once aspect of your work or personal life where your current system is not working properly. You can usually identify this type of problem because you keep having to do a work-around when things go wrong.

Two key words for identifying system failures are *always* and *never,* as in 'The invoices are *always* getting lost' or 'I can *never* keep up with my email'. Why are your invoices always getting lost and why can you never keep up with your email? – because you don't have good systems for dealing with them – that's why!

Once you have identified a system that is not working properly, start asking questions about it.

There will be more about systems in Chapter 4.

Putting it all together

We've spent two chapters now looking at what exactly productivity is and how it can be achieved. We've seen that true productivity is very different from most people's conception of it. It is not merely a matter of ploughing through as much work as possible, nor is it a matter of waiting around for inspiration to strike.

In the remainder of this part on the basics of productivity I will be explaining in more detail exactly how to apply the three components of productivity (Creativity, Efficiency and Consistency) to your life.

But before I do that, in the next chapter we will be looking at how you might ensure that you are *not* productive. We're not going to do that in order to guard ourselves from the ideas in the rest of this book, nor are we doing it in order to make ourselves less productive than we already are. The purpose of looking at how to be unproductive is because to be productive all we have to do is the opposite!

3 HOW TO BE UNPRODUCTIVE

Nothing is less productive than to make more efficient what should not be done at all.
Peter Drucker

I spent a lot of money on booze, girls and fast cars. The rest I just squandered.
George Best

Ladies, if a man says he will fix it, he will. There is no need to remind him every six months about it.
Anon

The hunter who chases two rabbits catches neither.
Chinese proverb

Being overwhelmed is often as unproductive as doing nothing, and is far more unpleasant. Being selective doing less is the path of the productive. Focus on the important few and ignore the rest.
Tim Ferriss

If you're reading this book, the chances are that you don't think that you are as productive as you'd like to be. But imagine that someone came to you and said 'I really admire how unproductive you are, O Great Teacher. Please teach me to be unproductive like you.' Well, you'd probably feel pretty upset by the question. But just think a minute – what would be the main points you'd make if you wanted to answer the question seriously?

You might come up with something like this:

Never say no to anyone

Pay no attention to developing good systems

Start lots of things which you don't finish

Do nothing to avoid distractions and interruptions

Avoid getting interested in what you are doing

Allow backlogs to build up

Leave stuff to the last minute and beyond

Think that you are naturally disorganized and there's nothing you can do about it

Follow the path of least resistance – go for what's easy rather than what's essential

Get submerged in trivial busy work

Have more commitments than you have time to complete

Don't ask for advice

Don't identify what's really important

When something goes wrong work round it instead of sorting it out

Make sure you forget important tasks by not writing them down

Take on so much work that you don't have time to concentrate on anything

Keep chopping and changing your priorities so nothing gets properly developed

Ensure that your most important work is constantly interrupted by trivial things going wrong because your low-level systems don't work properly

These points fall naturally under three headings:

> Be unsystematic
> Overload yourself
> Don't follow through

Let's have a look at each of these in turn (and please remember that these are what you should *avoid* doing if you want to be productive!).

1 BE UNSYSTEMATIC

The world 'unsystematic' has thoroughly deserved negative connotations. If we describe someone as unsystematic, we have in our mind the image of a person who takes action in fits and starts, is easily distracted and who can't be relied on. There may be occasions on which they produce good work because a burst of enthusiasm has given them enough forward impetus, but this quickly dies out and their lives are full of half-finished projects.

Often people are only unsystematic in part of their lives. For instance a singer may be very good at practising her art and developing her talent, but the rest of her life is in chaos. Unfortunately the part that is in chaos has a way of eventually impacting the artistic part.

A lack of consistency means that you are constantly moving from one thing to another without ever carrying anything through properly. This is very destructive to your work, and often to your relations with other people. People dislike working with people they perceive as being unreliable, and unfortunately it doesn't take much to persuade other people of the fact that you are unreliable. A few emails not replied to, a few broken promises of action, a few schemes in which you get other people involved and then let them down – all these leave their mark.

So being unsystematic is not just a matter of being a bit untidy. It is something that will potentially prevent your success at work and affect your relations with other people, both at work and in other areas of your life. In fact if there is one thing that distinguishes people who have happy and fulfilled lives from those that don't, it is probably the degree to which they are systematic and consistent. Not being able to rely on yourself is a very stressful and handicapping state to be in.

The good news is that it is actually very easy to become much more systematic. It is not a matter of personality but is a learned skill.

As an exercise, try and identify a few people in your life who you suspect consider you to be less than fully reliable. Can you identify what you might have done or failed to do which could have given them that impression?

2 OVERLOAD YOURSELF

Taking on too much is a very good way of ensuring that you are not going to be effective.

There is a basic mathematical rule about how much you can do. However much you try you can never get away from it. The rule is that one day's worth of incoming work must on average equal one day's outgoing work. This means that in theory you should be able to keep completely up-to-date with your work every day. In practice of course the amount of time available each day may vary, and your workload may vary too. But nevertheless, allowing for occasional peaks and troughs, you should be able to remain on top of your work just about all the time.

If this sounds like an impossible dream, then consider the fact that if you get behind on your work the reason can only be that you have more work coming in on average each day than you are capable of processing each day. How can you succeed in surviving at all if that is the case?

The answer is that some things will get done late, some things will be skimped and other things will not get done at all. Most people who have not balanced their workload keep their heads above water by a combination of all of these. There may be some things which do get done properly, but they are outweighed by the things that don't.

The point to note is that if you take on too much work, it is not some of your work that will suffer but *all* your work. Allowing your workload to get unbalanced in this way will affect everything you do, even seemingly quite unrelated areas. If for instance you are behind on several crucial projects at work, that is going to have an effect on your home life as well. Conversely if you don't allow enough time for exercise during your leisure time, that is eventually going to affect the energy you have available at work.

We all know the saying: 'If you want something done, ask a busy person'. Does this contradict what I have just been describing in this section?

Consider for a moment exactly what it is that makes you think that a busy person would be the best person to give a piece of work to? Do you give your work to them because they are overwhelmed by work and hardly able to keep up? Or because they are always missing deadlines because of the pressure of work? No, I don't think so. The truth is that it's not the fact that the person is busy that makes you think that they are a suitable person to trust with the work.

What you are actually looking for is a person who gets a lot done, yet is not behind in their work. The attractive quality is not that they are busy, but that they are effective. A person who is effective is better placed to take on new things than an ineffective person because they work more efficiently. Their effectiveness gives the correct impression that they are capable of doing and completing a lot more than most other people.

However the effective person knows that to take on too much is one of the finest ways of ensuring that one is no longer effective, so don't be surprised if they turn down your kind offer of work!

Both the effective and the ineffective person have exactly the same number of hours in the day. The difference is that the effective person gets more value out of those hours – and that is a cumulative effect. Becoming more efficient in one area opens up the time to bring other areas under control too.

3 DON'T FOLLOW THROUGH

To be unproductive all that is really needed is to fail to follow through on anything. You can work all the hours in the day, but if you never bring anything to fruition then you will be unproductive. Not following through is very easily done. All you need is to distract yourself constantly with new projects and new enthusiasms. Another good technique is to be too busy to work on a project for a few weeks, after which time you will have lost all the momentum which you built up earlier.

The effectiveness of a person should be judged not by how many projects they are working on, but by how many projects they have brought to fruition. Effective people can handle more projects than ineffective people simply because they are better organized, but they never allow themselves to take on so much that they can't keep up to date with everything.

If you compare the amount of work which productive and non-productive people do, you may be surprised to discover that non-productive people frequently put in more hours of work than productive people. This is because the productive person keeps up to date and therefore is not continually struggling to meet looming deadlines. They put in exactly the amount of work necessary to deliver comparatively few projects, while the unproductive person tends to work less time than is really needed on a comparatively large number of projects. The resulting pressure of partially completed projects causes them to work longer hours in total.

If the unproductive person is actually working longer hours than the productive person, then one can draw the perhaps surprising conclusion that lack of productiveness is not caused by laziness. It's more likely to be caused by working too hard on the wrong things and not hard enough on the right things.

Is it easier to be productive or unproductive?

Is it easier to be able to drive a car than not to be able to drive? Is it easier to be able to read than not to read? Is it easier to speak the language of the country you live in if you are an expat?

The answer is yes, it's much easier to be able to drive than have to beg lifts the whole time, to be able to read rather than to be illiterate, to speak the language rather than not be able to communicate. These are all learned skills and once you have acquired them they make life much easier.

In exactly the same way, being productive is a learned skill and once you have acquired it life becomes much easier. You are no longer being chased for deadlines the whole time, you can trust yourself to carry through on anything you want to or need to do, the ordinary business of life runs smoothly and you no longer have skeletons in the cupboard which you are afraid to look at.

Failing to learn the skills to be productive puts you in the same position as people who have never learned to drive, or have never learned to read or have never learned to speak to the local people in their own language. Life is more difficult because you haven't acquired the skill. Your lack of the skill is a definite handicap.

To overcome the handicap you need to acquire the skill. In the case of learning to read, learning to drive or learning a foreign language, this can be quite daunting. Fortunately learning productivity skills is relatively easy compared with these, and the rewards are at least as great. On the other hand, just as it's very easy to continue not to learn to read, drive a car, or learn the local language, so it's very easy to continue to be ineffective and unproductive.

The title of this chapter is 'How to Be Unproductive'. What have we learned about it?

If you are reading this book you are probably already feel that you are unproductive to a greater or lesser degree, otherwise you wouldn't find it necessary to be reading it. So if you want to be more unproductive then all you have to do is basically more of the same – don't bother about developing any new systems, take on even more commitments than you have already and hop from subject to subject without properly finishing anything. It is indeed very easy.

The good news is that it's equally easy to move in the opposite direction and become more productive. Learn how to improve your systems, weed out your commitments and make sure things are followed through to completion and beyond. The rest of this book will help you with each of these.

Remember though that you don't need to become perfect overnight. Even a small move in the right direction will make a lot of difference.

4 THINK SYSTEMS

*Civilization advances by extending the number of
important operations which we can perform
without thinking about them.*
Alfred North Whitehead

For every minute spent in organizing, an hour is earned.
Benjamin Franklin

*The founding fathers were not only brilliant, they were system
builders and systematic thinkers. They came up with
comprehensive plans and visions.*
Ron Chernow

*Being busy does not always mean real work. The object of all
work is production or accomplishment and to either of
these ends there must be forethought, system, planning,
intelligence, and honest purpose, as well as perspiration.
Seeming to do is not doing.*
Thomas A. Edison

To err is human; to manage error is system.
Kevin Kelly

The difference between productive people and unproductive
people is very largely a matter of developing the right systems.
We tend to think that the fact that our work or our home life
is disorganized is because we are a 'disorganized person' –
something we are born with and which we can't change. Whereas
in truth we are simply a person who is using the wrong systems.
It's our systems which are letting us down, not we ourselves.

Relying on will power is not going to work in the long term. For
lasting results, what we have to aim for is to make it easier to do
the right thing than to do the wrong thing. So above all a good

system must be *easy* to keep to. If it's difficult we are never going to stick to it.

Systems come in a hierarchy. At the lowest level we have systems for the normal day-to-day activities which no one can avoid unless they are in the fortunate position of having plenty of servants or staff to do the work for them. Even then it's important to make sure that the servants and staff are using the right systems. For most of us these low-level systems cover such things as processing paper, email and other incoming communications, paying bills, issuing invoices, filing and the myriad minor tasks which come up all the time.

If you don't have these basics covered, then you will always be held back. You can't afford to be spending time on an inefficient system for email or struggling to get your tax return in by the due date – these take up time which you should be spending on productive work.

Good systems for simple administration will free your mind for more productive work. Ideally you shouldn't need to have to think about the lower-level stuff at all. Thinking needs to be kept for the high-level systems, which will be designed to fit each particular case. But even then the aim of designing a high-level system is to avoid eventually having to think about that system too. For instance, if you are writing a book, once you have designed and implemented your systems for writing it, you can stop thinking about them and concentrate on the writing itself. In the case of writing a book there might be a hierarchy of systems something like this:

Time management system

Systems for ensuring basic working/writing needs, e.g. refreshments, computing, heating, back-up, etc

System for daily writing, e.g. when, how, how much

System for writing method, e.g. research, first draft, editing

When designing a system, remember that we as human beings have a natural tendency to follow *the path of least resistance*, that is to say when we are given a choice between doing something difficult and something easier we will always tend to go for the easier thing. In doing this we are simply acting like the rest of nature. A swamp and a river are very different things but they are both made up of water. In both the swamp and the river the water is just doing what water does. What makes the difference is that a river has banks and is going somewhere while a swamp doesn't have banks and is going nowhere.

A good system is like the river banks which guide your actions and direction. When the banks are in place they form the path of least resistance, just like the river which flows downhill to the sea. When you design a system your aim should be to make following it the path of least resistance. That means it must be easy to keep to.

To take a very simple example, it's much easier to keep things tidy if you know where everything is supposed to go. When you know what to do with something, then the path of least resistance is to do exactly that. When there is no system and you don't know what to do with something then the path of least resistance is usually to leave it for later – and later never comes!

1 PAY ATTENTION TO THE KEY WORDS *ALWAYS* AND *NEVER*

A sure sign of an unsatisfactory system is when you find yourself complaining about something going wrong and using the words *always* and *never*. Here are some examples of what I mean:

I'm *always* behind on my email

They *never* remember to bring the milk in the morning

I can *never* get this thing to work properly

I'm *always* forgetting to check my schedule in the morning

When you hear yourself saying something like this, a red flag should go up in your mind. You have a systems failure.

The characteristic of a systems failure is that it goes on and on producing the wrong result, hence the words *always* and *never*. It's not a one-off mistake – it's something which keeps on producing the wrong thing.

Faced with something that goes on and on producing the wrong result, you'd think that the easiest thing to do would be to put it right. Unfortunately this is not the case.

The problem is that each time the system goes wrong we don't consider the cumulative effect of continually producing the wrong result. We only look at that particular incident. When we do that, the path of least resistance is to work round what has gone wrong, rather than to use more effort and fix the system for good and all. This is why we can put up with faulty systems for years on end.

Of course if we do succeed in putting in the effort to sort it out for good and all, we are going to save huge amounts of time and effort in the future.

2 YOU ALREADY HAVE A SYSTEM – TAKE A LOOK AT WHAT IT IS

It sounds very obvious but one of the reasons people get stuck in poor systems is that they never take the trouble to examine what they are already doing.

Did you catch the word *never* there? Yes, this is an example of a systems failure. It's a failure in the system for putting systems right.

We need to look at systems in a purely functional way. Systems are not moral entities. There is no such thing as a 'good' system or a 'bad' system. All we can say is that there are systems which produce different results. Every system is a perfect system for producing the results which it produces.

If you are using a system and don't like the results you are getting, it's not because you are using a 'bad' system. It's because you are using a system which produces different results from the results you want. If you want a tidy office but the system you are using produces an untidy office, then you are using the wrong system for the result you want.

The system you are using produces the results you are getting. To get different results you need a different system. You will not get different results without looking at *why* your existing system produces the existing results. Remember, there's nothing wrong with the system – it unfailingly produces the results it was designed to produce. It's just that we don't want those results so we need a different system.

I will give a very simple example here, relating to something which just about all of us are involved in. This is email. Not everyone has a problem with email but problems are sufficiently common to make it a good example. We often hear people say 'I'm *always* struggling with my email' or 'I can *never* catch up with my backlog'. It's a pervasive problem, and it means that one's energy and time are constantly being sucked away by email, rather than being employed more productively. It is a fine example of a lower-level system going wrong.

Now of course there are lots of reasons why people find it difficult to keep up with email, but as a first step let's just examine the system the average person might use to deal with email:

Check email

Ten emails have arrived

Deal with five of them

Leave the rest for later

The figures will vary of course, but you only have to look at it to see that this system will automatically result in a backlog of email. It's very efficient at doing just that. It is in fact a perfect system for producing a backlog – it would be hard to design a better one.

The trouble is that you don't want a backlog of email. So what would be a system for *not* producing a backlog? Answer: virtually any system would be better than the current one. If you don't want a backlog, then the last thing you want to be using is a perfect system for producing a backlog.

3 ASK QUESTIONS ABOUT THE SYSTEM

Once you've taken a look at your present system, it may be abundantly obvious what the problem with it is. To take the email example, it's clear that only dealing with five emails out of ten with no plan for dealing with the other five (except 'leaving them for later') is the key issue.

However it's important not to stop there, and you need to question the system further. Remember that questioning is one of the top characteristics of productive people (see Chapter 1). In the case of the email you might question each of the stages, e.g.

How often should I check email?

Why am I getting so much email? How can I reduce it?

What is stopping me dealing with all ten emails, instead of five?

How can I specify when I will deal with emails which I can't deal with immediately?

You can no doubt think of other questions. It's not until you ask the questions that you are going to be able to come up with ideas.

I'm not going to tell you what a better email system would be for you. If you question the situation properly you should be able to come up with one yourself.

In other situations some useful all-purpose questions are:

Where is this going wrong?

How could it be done more quickly?

Does it need to be done by me?

Does it need to be done at all?

There's more about asking questions in the next two chapters (5 and 6).

Putting it all together

As an exercise try to design a better email system for yourself. If email is not a problem for you, then use another low-level system which is giving you trouble.

Once you've designed the better system, try it out and then adjust it from your experience. Remember that you are aiming to make it *easier* to do it right than to do it wrong.

It's a good idea to make a list of all your low-level systems and then make sure that they are all working well. Remember the test is how much you have to think about the system once it is in operation. The sign of a good system is that you hardly have to think about it at all.

Everything I've said about low-level systems applies to high-level systems as well. In fact there's no cut-and-dried distinction between a low-level system and a high-level system. It's all a matter of degree. Low-level systems are the routine tasks that one deals with on a daily or weekly basis (sometimes monthly or annually). High-level systems are what are used in new projects and developments.

When you start on a new project, you need to design the systems by which you are going to work on the project. Failure to get this right can mean that you are constantly being tripped up by things going wrong. This is especially important as high-level systems frequently involve other people, sometimes large numbers of them.

5 REPEATED QUESTIONING

It requires a very unusual mind to undertake the analysis of the obvious.
Alfred North Whitehead

It is not the answer that enlightens, but the question.
Eugene Ionesco

The only stupid question is the one that is not asked.
English proverb

In all affairs it's a healthy thing now and then to hang a question mark on the things you have long taken for granted.
Bertrand Russell

The wise man doesn't give the right answers, he poses the right questions.
Claude Levi-Strauss

Questioning is fundamental to the creative process. The story of Isaac Newton and the apple may be apocryphal, but it wasn't until he asked '*Why* do things fall downwards?' – something everyone had taken for granted – that the Theory of Gravity could be formulated. This question built on the earlier question asked by Galileo: 'Do heavier objects fall faster than lighter objects?' Until that question had been asked everyone had just assumed that heavier objects fall faster – an assumption that turned out to be wrong.

Once you have formulated a question it leads naturally to further questions. All these questions then lead to experiments, research or new ideas.

A questioning attitude is fundamental to the productive person. Why not be like Newton and keep a list of questions? Write them down, and don't worry if they seem obvious. It's often by questioning the obvious that new ideas are born.

At the heart of the questioning attitude is the simple psychological fact that once the mind has been asked a question it tries to answer it. The more times the question is asked the more the mind tries to answer it.

Often the answer to a question is another question. I referred a moment ago to Galileo's question 'Do heavier objects fall faster than lighter objects?' Galileo's answer to this question was 'How can I find out?' The result was his famous experiment from the top of the Leaning Tower of Pisa.

The most useful questions for being creative are those beginning with 'why?' and 'how?'.

These may need to be supplemented by other more informational questions like 'what?', 'when?', 'where?' and 'who?'. Nevertheless it's 'why?' and 'how?' which will result in the real creative process.

1 ASK 'WHY' QUESTIONS

It's much more effective to ask questions than to make statements. If for instance you notice that your garage door isn't working properly, you would probably ignore it for a time and then eventually write down a note to 'Fix the garage door'. Or you might simply write 'Garage door not working'.

The creative person would do it differently. They would write down something like 'Why isn't the garage door working properly?' Note something very important about this. It is far less threatening than the action command 'Fix the garage door', which suggests hard work, yet it leads naturally to further investigation – unlike 'Garage door not working' (to which the subconscious answer is 'So what?')

'Why isn't the garage door working properly?' leads to investigation and further questions, such as 'What can I do about it?', 'What sort of door would work better?' or even 'Why am I using the garage for storage instead of keeping my car in it?' The final result may be quite different from what would happen if you had written 'Fix the garage door'.

To go back to the email example in the previous chapter, your initial thought could be 'I can't keep up with my email'. This might prompt the question 'Why can't I keep up with my email?' You will come up with various answers to this question which you can turn into questions as well. 'I'm getting too much email' might become 'Why am I getting so much email?' and then 'What would be the right amount of email for me to be getting?' or 'How can I reduce the amount of email I am getting?'

Instead of the statement 'I can't keep up with my email', which is really nothing more than a complaint, posing it as the question 'Why can't I keep up with my email?' should result in some definite improvements in how you handle your email.

2 FOLLOW UP WITH 'HOW?' QUESTIONS

'Why?' questions are essential, but need to result in 'How?' questions. And sometimes 'How?' questions will lead back to 'Why?' questions. Galileo's experiment on the Leaning Tower of Pisa was in answer to the question '*How* can I find out whether heavy objects fall at the same rate as lighter objects?' The results of the experiment led naturally to the question '*Why* do heavy objects fall at the same rate as lighter objects?'

As an experiment, have a look around your office until you spot something that is not the way you'd like it to be. It might be a pile of paper that needs filing. It might be a cracked windowpane. It might be anything. Then ask the question: 'Why is that paper unfiled?' or 'Why has that cracked windowpane not been replaced yet?' Once you've answered that question see how many 'How?' questions come out of your answer. For example you might ask 'How can I get rid of that pile of paper?' or 'How can I ensure that windowpane is replaced quickly?'

A question like 'Why is that paper unfiled?' is very different from saying 'I need to file those papers'. The reason the paper is unfiled is not because you are lazy. It's because your system for filing papers is deficient. Asking a 'Why?' question then leads naturally into the sort of 'How?' questions that result in a new and better system.

3 ASK THE SAME QUESTION REPEATEDLY

One technique which can be very effective is to ask the same question repeatedly. Whenever a question is repeated it tends to start off a new train of thought in our minds. For example here is an exchange I had with myself about the importance of questioning in creativity.

> *What is the importance to a productive person of asking questions?*

First and foremost because productivity rarely involves doing things in the way they have always been done. The productive person needs to think of new ways to do things, question what purpose is served by ongoing practices and change them where and when necessary.

This doesn't however imply change for change's sake. Changing things unnecessarily is usually the result of a lack of good questioning. It is a substitute for effective action. The desire for novelty should be resisted at all costs. What we are looking for is not novelty but productivity.

> *What is the importance to a productive person of asking questions?*

Questioning is an important psychological attitude. It means the mind is open to new ideas without accepting them uncritically. It's also important psychologically because asking a question invites an answer. Sometimes the question needs to be asked more than once before getting to the root of the matter. Sometimes one question leads to further questions. And sometimes the answer to one question gives a new aspect to the answers already given to a different question.

Questioning is therefore important for growing one's brain. It encourages the development of links within the brain, which is literal physical growth in the brain. If you ask enough questions about a subject, you will form enough links within your brain for a new perspective to emerge.

This can take time. I expect everyone has had the experience of putting aside a piece of work for a day or so (or even a few hours) and finding that they have many new thoughts about it.

What is the importance to a productive person of asking questions?

There are many ways in which one can ask questions, and I intend to devote the next chapter to some of them, but the essential thing is not how you ask questions but that you ask them. Furthermore, asking yourself questions implies that you will also ask other people questions. Provided they are asked in a non-threatening way and you are showing real interest most people respond well to questions.

In this example I asked the same question three times, but I could easily have asked it more times and still have found that I had something to add. To go deeper, you can repeat the exercise the following day and answer it without referring to what you wrote before.

By the way, if you try this exercise for yourself and are typing the answers, type the question out in full each time too. Don't just copy and paste it.

The sort of questioning which productive people use seems to be in rather short supply in today's world. We find instead that the majority of people, including those in positions of high authority, seem to have two main methods of dealing with situations.

The first is to follow the prevailing fashion or orthodoxy without questioning it at all. As the fashion changes so does people's thinking, which is really little more than an automatic response to certain stimuli.

The second is to react to problems by throwing away everything, whether it works or not, and producing something entirely new. Usually it's not just new, but also untried.

In terms of our own lives, these equate to:

1. Living mainly in response to other people's demands or expectations without every really taking the time to think about what we are doing
2. Throwing over what we are doing in response to the latest enthusiasm

Productive people on the other hand are not attempting to overthrow the past but to build on it. They recognize that following fashions and prevailing orthodoxies is a substitute for thought, and that these things need to be questioned like everything else.

In the next chapter, I shall be giving some further techniques for asking questions and getting great answers.

6 HOW TO GET GREAT IDEAS

*An idea that is not dangerous is unworthy of being
called an idea at all.*

Oscar Wilde

*That's the great secret of creativity. You treat ideas like cats:
you make them follow you.*

Ray Bradbury

*The way to get good ideas is to get lots of ideas and throw
the bad ones away.*

Linus Pauling

No man was ever wise by chance.

Seneca

*An idea is a point of departure and no more. As soon as you
elaborate it, it becomes transformed by thought.*

Pablo Picasso

As we've seen in the previous section, when you ask your mind
a question it starts to work on the answer. We've also seen that
an effective technique for encouraging our mind to do this is to
ask the question repeatedly. Every time the mind comes to a halt,
repeating the question starts a new train of thought.

We've also touched on the fact that repeating this sort of exercise
the following day can produce further insights into the question.
This effect is known as 'maturation' and means that the mind has
been working subconsciously on the question even while we are
occupied with other things. This maturation effect also applies
to such things as practising a musical instrument, learning a
language or writing an article. All of them benefit from being put

aside for a period of about a day and then taken up again. After a night's sleep the brain has had time to absorb and integrate the subject. I'll be dealing more with this effect in Chapter 8.

Now I'm going to describe some additional effective techniques which use questioning and maturation. This is not intended to be a comprehensive list. There are many more possible ways. You may be able to discover some. How? By asking questions of course!

1 THE FIVE BEST IDEAS

This is my favourite method for generating new ideas. You can use it for almost any subject, even for thinking up the best questions to ask.

All you have to do is write the question 'What are my five best ideas for [the subject you want to generate ideas for]?' So you might write:

What are my five best ideas for the publicity campaign?

What are my five best ideas for this year's holiday?

What are my five best ideas for my mother's birthday present?

Then write down underneath the question five answers off the top of your head. At this stage don't worry too much about how good the answers are, as long as you get five down. There is no need to spend a long time thinking about the answers. It is best just to write down the first five things that come into your head.

Put the answers away somewhere where you can't see them, and repeat the exercise again the following day. Don't refer to your previous answers. It doesn't matter whether your answers this time were on yesterday's list or not.

Do this exercise for five days or so and then examine all the answers you have written and compare them.

2 ANSWERING A QUESTION THAT NEEDS THOUGHT

This exercise is similar to the first one, but in this case there is no fixed limit to the number of answers you give, though you are recommended to aim for about ten or twelve. As in the first exercise you ask yourself the question daily for five days or so and then compare the answers.

You can use it for virtually any subject which requires thought on your part. Some examples:

What are the most important things I need to concentrate on this year?

What would be my ideal job?

What would I really, really like to do?

How can I increase the turnover of my business?

How can I get over my fear of making sales calls?

If I had no fear, what would I do?

This takes slightly longer than the previous exercise but it does have the advantage of stretching one's mind to a greater extent. When the mind is stretched it is more likely to continue thinking deeply about the subject in between sessions.

3 THINKING WITH BULLET POINTS

A method which I use a lot myself, especially when I am out and about with only a smartphone for company, is thinking with bullet points. I just jot down more or less random thoughts without any attempt to make a coherent narrative out of them. Each thought is a separate bullet point. The great advantage of this is that it can be done in almost any circumstances – on a bus, in a train, doing the shopping, childminding – any time you can snatch a moment or two to jot down a thought.

The effect of doing this is to generate more thoughts. Quite a considerable number of bullet points can be generated in a short time. Not all will be of equal value of course, so it's important to go back through the thoughts, preferably after a few hours, and select the most valuable ones.

Here's an example of a session which someone might have carried out on the subject of time management.

- Still not happy with my time management system.
- I don't seem to get enough done as far as quantity is concerned.
- I would like a method in which the small stuff gets progressed faster.
- I don't know how to do that.
- I suppose I could have a section called minor tasks and progress it just like email and paper etc, one pass at a time.
- Stuff has to be dealt with in one go and must not recur the same day.
- So that could include some of the stuff which I put on the main list at the moment.
- Why have the restriction about recurring? Just must be done in one go.
- Should go on pretty early in the day.

Note that there's no attempt to make a logical argument. Some bullet points follow others logically and others don't. It's not written for an external audience. What is written is meaningful to the person writing it, but not necessarily to anyone else.

Putting it all together

You may find when you succeed in generating some good ideas with these methods that you will almost automatically start taking action on the best of them. You don't necessarily need to wait to complete the exercise before deciding which are the best ideas. Allow this process of moving into action to happen. It's a very natural process and you don't want to get in its way. Your mind is beginning to integrate the ideas fully and it's natural for it to seek expression in action.

Once you start taking action on an idea, you will find that more new ideas and perspectives arrive as a result. You may then want to keep re-running the exercise to expand the ideas further. There is a whole cycle of achievement here. Questioning leads to the brain generating new ideas, new ideas generate further ideas, the brain seeks to express the ideas through action and action generates yet further ideas as you move forward.

7 LITTLE AND OFTEN

A great deal of talent is lost to the world for want of a little courage. Every day sends to their graves obscure men whose timidity prevented them from making a first effort.
Sydney Smith

When you improve a little each day, eventually big things occur. When you improve conditioning a little each day, eventually you have a big improvement in conditioning. Not tomorrow, not the next day, but eventually a big gain is made. Don't look for the big, quick improvement. Seek the small improvement one day at a time. That's the only way it happens – and when it happens, it lasts.
John Wooden

All changes, even positive ones, are scary. Attempts to reach goals through radical or revolutionary means often fail because they heighten fear.
Robert Maurer

Whoever wants to reach a distant goal must take small steps.
Helmut Schmidt

In the book you'll find lots of encouragement to pick up a pen or pencil and make a small drawing of something right in front of you. And if you keep doing one little drawing at a time, you'll eventually have a book full of drawings of your life.
Michael Nobbs, Drawing Your Life

One of the major causes of procrastination is that we tend to look at an entire project and terrify ourselves with the huge size of it. Yet just about every project will respond to a technique known as 'little and often'.

'Little and often' is one of the fundamental ways in which the human mind acts – not only the human mind, but also the human body. Every major talent relies on 'little and often', whether it's ability to play a musical instrument, athletic prowess, writing books, building a business, learning a foreign language, gardening, or even keeping a house clean and tidy.

The most important thing to remember about 'little and often' is that with both mental and physical training the improvement actually takes place in the gaps between sessions. If it's a mental ability the brain makes the connections when you are not working on the project. If it's a physical ability, exactly the same happens with the body. It responds to the exercise session during the period before the next session. The problem with both mental and physical activities is that the improvement will start to fade if the gap is too long.

The 'often' from 'little and often' is a relative term. It can refer to anything between a few minutes rest and three or four days. Anything above that, and the improvement tends to die away. It's quite possible for instance to play a sport once a week for years without seeing much improvement. The reason is that a week is just about long enough for the improvement caused by your session to fade back to where you were before. This is also the reason why it's essential to do some work between your weekly language classes. Even a couple of hours' revision midway through the week can make the difference between progressing and stagnating.

'Little' is also a relative term here. It is the opposite of 'do it all in one big session at the last minute'. For some things that could be a matter of a few minutes. For a concert pianist daily practice could be as long as four hours. For an author it could be two or three hours work.

Saving it all up for one big session at the last minute has a lot of disadvantages. These include:

> The size of the session causes resistance and procrastination
> There is no 'maturation' effect (see previous chapter)

If something else comes up at the last minute, you are likely to miss your deadline.

If it is a continuing project then there will not be much improvement because of the fading effect.

In every respect then, whether it's overcoming procrastination, quality of work, ease of scheduling, or speed of improvement, 'little and often' wins out.

1 OVERCOMING PROCRASTINATION AND RESISTANCE

Most techniques for overcoming procrastination are based on 'little and often'. The resistance we feel to getting going on an unpleasant task or large project is usually due to looking at it as a whole, rather than as a series of steps. Once we make a start it usually then becomes easy to continue to make progress. However don't forget that 'often' is just as important as 'little'. If we make a start on something and then don't follow it up with further action, we will find that resistance builds up again. Making a habit of working 'little and often' can have the effect of removing procrastination from our lives more or less completely. Considering the very damaging effect that procrastination can have, that is a huge benefit.

Some common anti-procrastination techniques based on 'little and often' are as follows:

Salami slicing

This technique relies on identifying the first step for a big project. You should make the step small enough for you to be able to do it without resistance. So for instance if you have been putting off writing an important report, your first step might be 'Write an outline of the report'. Unfortunately this might still be too large for you, in which case you might go for something really elementary such as 'Open a file for the report'. Once you've done the first step you may find that further steps can be larger since you will have gained some momentum.

I'll just get the file out

This is similar to salami slicing but a little bit more 'psychological'. It relies on tricking yourself to get started by using the following sentence: 'I'm not really going to write the report now, but I'll just get the file out'. Once you have got the file out, nine times out of ten you will go on to do some more work on the report. You can use this for all sorts of situations, e.g.

'I'm not really going to mow the lawn now, but I'll just get the lawnmower out'

'I'm not really going to go for a three-mile run now, but I'll just change into my running kit'

'I'm not really going to ring that angry customer now, but I'll just look up his phone number'

These two techniques of 'Salami slicing' and 'I'll just get the file out' are only examples and there are many more ways you can use the 'little and often' principle to overcome procrastination. But really just getting into the habit of working little and often on everything you have to do, apart from the most trivial tasks, is the best way of avoiding procrastination altogether. You won't need emergency techniques like these once you have made little and often the basis of your working practice.

2 GETTING YOUR MIND WORKING TO PRODUCE HIGHER-QUALITY WORK

I've mentioned the maturation effect in Chapter 6. Maturation is the effect by which the mind works on something in the background even when you are not thinking about it consciously. Therefore when you come back to the subject after a short break you will find that your understanding of the subject will have moved on.

This is another major advantage to working 'little and often'. Not only do you overcome procrastination and make the work far easier, but you also produce higher-quality work.

As an example, if you are reading a report and come to a part which you have difficulty understanding, just leave it and continue with the rest of the report. Then come back to it after a break and you may well find that it has become much clearer.

If you've ever re-read a book that you first read several years before you will probably have experienced the maturation effect on a longer scale. The contents mean much more to you than they did at first reading because you have made many more connections in your mind since then.

3 SPEED UP OR SLOW DOWN ACCORDING TO CIRCUMSTANCES

Let's take the example of writing a report. When someone is given a deadline which is a month away, there is a strong tendency to leave the report until the deadline is looming. So out of the thirty possible days on which work on the report could have been done only about three or four are actually used. The results are predictable. The writing of the report is rushed. There isn't enough research. There's no maturation effect. Any last-minute emergencies which come up may throw the whole thing off. And finally the stress on the writer is considerable.

The simple answer to this is that when you are given a piece of work with a deadline you should start work on it right away – however far off the deadline is.

If you do this with all your work you will find that you accomplish exactly the same amount – or more – without all the stress and rush associated with leaving things to the last minute. The quality of the work will be higher and you will be able to accommodate things like genuine emergencies far more easily.

What's more, if the deadline gets shifted, something that frequently happens, then you can respond easily just by changing the frequency of your sessions on the report.

Putting it all together

'Little and often' is a powerful tool. As an exercise, spend a couple of minutes jotting down anything in your life at present which you think might benefit from this approach.

A few suggestions:

Learning a language

Practising a sport

Playing a musical instrument

Writing an article or report

Doing research

Dealing with email

Then pick one, decide what would be an appropriate number and frequency of sessions and go ahead. For most subjects once a day is usually best, but you will probably want to deal with your email several times a day. With sports and other physical training you should avoid doing the same type of intensive activity more often than once every two days as otherwise minor injuries can build up without giving the body time to recover from them.

8 THE VALUE OF DISCRETIONARY TIME

Regret for wasted time is more wasted time.
Mason Cooley

*Time is more valuable than money. You can get more money,
but you cannot get more time.*
Jim Rohn

*Time is really the only capital that any human being has, and
the only thing he can't afford to lose.*
Thomas Edison

The bad news is time flies. The good news is you're the pilot.
Michael Altshuler

*Time equals life; therefore, waste your time and waste your
life, or master your time and master your life.*
Alan Lakein

For the productive person discretionary time is essential and
needs to be closely guarded.

What do I mean by 'discretionary time'? I mean time during
which you have a choice of what you can do. It may not be
a wide choice, but it is to some degree a choice. If you are an
employee who works in an office you may not have a choice
about being in the office and there may be a limited range
of activities you can do while you're there. But within those
limitations you have a choice. You can be answering email,
writing a report, phoning a client, or any other work-related
task. To put it simply, discretionary time is when you are working
off a list rather than off a schedule.

Some jobs have hardly any discretionary time. For example, if you are a cashier in a bank or an assistant in a busy shop, your job is simply to deal with the next customer. Of course you can still concentrate on improving the efficiency with which you do this. Being more efficient will make life easier both for yourself and for your customers and may lead to promotion.

Generally speaking the higher you rise in an organization the more discretionary time you will have and the wider the choice of what you can do in that time will be. A senior manager usually has more control over their time than a junior manager, and a junior manager than someone in a non-managerial post.

The opposite of discretionary time is non-discretionary time. Non-discretionary time is time in which we have no control over what we are doing. For someone in a managerial post, non-discretionary time would include meetings, seminars, sales events and such-like. These are usually, though not always, pre-scheduled.

Think of non-discretionary time as being the appointments and meetings entered in your diary, while discretionary time is the white space that surrounds them.

Although this chapter is about the value of discretionary time, I'm not saying that discretionary time is good and non-discretionary time is bad. Far from it. Non-discretionary time is essential. It includes planning, client meetings, learning and other activities which are part and parcel of being productive. In many jobs non-discretionary time is when the core work is actually done.

What is at issue is the balance between discretionary and non-discretionary time. The purpose of most meetings is to agree and allocate work. When is that work going to be done? Much of it in our discretionary time. If we over-schedule ourselves then we are leaving ourselves no time to deal with it.

Although we don't have a choice about what we are doing during non-discretionary time, we do often have some control of how many meetings and other items of non-discretionary time we schedule. Scheduling wall-to-wall meetings simply defeats the purpose of having meetings because you leave yourself no time to process and action the points coming out of the meetings.

In addition to over-scheduling, another thing to watch out for is non-productive meetings. These are one of the biggest time killers in many work places. Frequently meetings can take on a life of their own, and therefore the purpose of all regular meetings should be kept under review. We don't want to fall into the stereotype of managers who spend all their time in meetings in which the only thing decided is the date of the next meeting. All meetings should be cost-effective in terms of the results that they generate.

1 TREAT YOUR DISCRETIONARY TIME AS A PRECIOUS RESOURCE

For productive people, discretionary time is one of their most valuable resources. This is the time in which they are going to ask questions, develop new ideas, design routines and systems, and apply them to the work. Giving discretionary time away unnecessarily is something they avoid at all costs.

If you want to become a more productive person, be like them. Don't give discretionary time away lightly. It is the time in which you will be doing most of the work which goes towards your productivity.

A word of warning. Discretionary time is not just potentially the most productive time you have, it is also the time which is easiest to waste. You can spend your time doing productive work in a productive way. Alternatively you can spend your time rushing after one deadline or another in a constant state of stress. In the worst case you can just fritter the time away surfing the net, replying to your Facebook friends and immersing yourself in busy work in an attempt to avoid the things you don't want to do.

2 MANAGE NON-DISCRETIONARY TIME

Because of the adverse effects of overloading yourself with meetings and appointments it is essential that you take the management of non-discretionary time very seriously. You may not have any discretion over what you do during non-discretionary time, but you do usually have at least some discretion over how much non-discretionary time you book into your diary. You need to control it as far as you are able to.

Don't forget that meetings and appointments may take up far more time than it would appear from looking at your diary. You have to prepare for them, they may involve travel, and you may come away from them with a lot of work. Conferences and seminars are even worse time consumers which may take up whole days at a time.

This doesn't mean that you shouldn't ever book yourself into a conference or seminar. These can be very useful learning experiences and chances to meet influential people in your line of work. But what you must be alert to is that you need to make sure that every meeting or event is a good use of your time. I don't mean a good use of your time in the abstract, but a good use of your time compared to what you would have succeeded in achieving during the discretionary time which it is supplanting.

3 DISTANT ELEPHANTS

An analogy often used by time management teachers is that of a distant herd of elephants seen from the top of a ridge in Kenya. At that distance they seem very peaceful and quiet. That's a very different experience from finding your path blocked by an angry elephant a hundred yards away which is stamping its foot and trumpeting at you.

This is like the way that you look at the pages of your diary. In six months' time, it seems to be very empty. There's lots of white space with nothing in it. So if you get an invitation to attend a conference or seminar, it seems to fit very easily into that white space without disturbing anything. Like the herd of elephants it seems very peaceful and quiet at that distance.

But of course this is an illusion. The white space in your diary is not empty at all. It is full of all the stuff you usually do. And when it gets to the day before that conference which you so easily fitted into all that white space, it will be like the angry elephant stamping its foot at you.

The moral of this is that whenever you are about to book yourself into something in what seems to be the distant uncluttered future, think what it is going to be like the day before. You will have tons of work to do and will be cursing the day you ever thought it was a good idea to go on this conference.

Putting it all together

As an exercise, look at your diary for the next full week (i.e. Monday to Friday if that is your working week) and work out how much time out of your normal working hours you are scheduled to spend in meetings or travelling to meetings. Include conference calls and anything else which represents non-discretionary time. Then work out how much your week will be divided between discretionary and non-discretionary time. Spend some time reflecting on the balance between the two. Have you left enough discretionary time to deal with the work? Are all the appointments and meetings in your diary for the week worthwhile activities?

Put your findings away and make a note to look at them again at the end of the week which you have just analysed. How far did what actually happen during the week resemble what you had scheduled? How did the balance between discretionary and non-discretionary time work out in practice? Was the balance different? If so, which gained at the expense of the other? Were newly scheduled meetings and appointments worthwhile and necessary? Did any relate to emergencies which could have been prevented at an earlier stage?

9 PRODUCTIVE TIME MANAGEMENT

The question is not whether something is high priority or low priority, but whether it should be done at all.
Mark Forster

Much of the stress that people feel doesn't come from having too much to do. It comes from not finishing what they've started.
David Allen

There is no such thing as time management. There is only the mindset that optimally manages the self and its actions.
Tony Dovale

Take climbing a mountain. Which step matters most? The first? The last? That one right in the middle? The odd-numbered ones? Weren't they all necessary?
Khatzumoto

The secret to living your life to its potential is to value the important stuff above your own comfort.
Brian P. Moran

One of the basic systems we need is how to manage our time. If this is wrong then everything else is going to be wrong too. There are hundreds of different possible systems. I've written about several in my previous books and experimented with a lot more on my blog at www.markforster.net.

Ideally the productive person needs a system which is going to be based on the productivity principles which I've described, particularly the questioning methods and 'little and often'. It should fulfil the following essential requirements:

Basic daily routines should be under control

Tasks should be actioned quickly and systematically

Big projects should be given adequate time.

Furthermore the system should be robust enough for the person using it to be able to maintain the integrity of the system without continually having to adjust and amend it. Any good system should operate in the background with a minimum of time spent on system administration.

1 THROW AWAY YOUR TO-DO LIST

I can almost hear the gasps of dismay when I say 'Throw away your to-do list'. And not just your to-do list, but also your list of daily priorities, your project list, your weekly list and your someday/maybe list if you maintain one.

The problem with to-do lists is that they are basically out of date within a very short time after you've written them. They are records of what you might have done or could have done at a point of time which is already receding into the past. They bear little relationship to what it's actually possible or desirable to be doing in the present. What's worse, to-do lists have a strong tendency to expand faster than you can do the work on them. The result of this is that they add to your stress by making you feel that you are permanently behind on your work without any prospect of ever catching up.

In a moment I am going to propose a system which does not rely on lists, is always up-to-date with your present situation, never expands beyond what you can actually do and encourages you to work little and often on the things that really matter. But first I want to say a little about the importance of maintaining focus in your work.

2 KEEP A NARROW FOCUS

The natural tendency of to-do lists is to diversify your attention over an ever wider range of subjects. This is exactly the opposite of what you need. You need a time management system which concentrates your attention on what is really important.

This is not easy to achieve because, as well as the natural tendency of to-do lists to expand, we are also up against our own natural tendency to overuse a good system when we find one. If we start using a time management system which works better than our current one, instead of using it to concentrate and deepen our work we use it to take on more work. Eventually of course however good the system it will collapse under the strain. Virtually any system can be destroyed by overloading it.

There is another factor which makes it difficult to keep a narrow focus. I became very aware of this when I was giving seminars and coaching individuals in time management. This factor is that many people are very protective of their workloads. It's almost as if being overly busy is an important element of their self-image.

Anyone who wants to be a productive person needs to get rid of this attitude. Our self-image should be based on the fact that we are productive, not that we are busy.

The fact is that however busy we may consider ourselves to be, we cannot do more work than we can fit into the 24 hours that we are issued with every day. Of course there's a lot of things besides work that have to be fitted into the day as well. To-do lists mislead us by giving us the impression that we can do more than can be fitted into 24 hours. The result is an inevitable backlog of tasks and projects, which will either end up being abandoned or skimped.

Narrow focus is based on the idea that you only take on work if you are able to keep up to date with it. As we've seen in an earlier chapter, the ideal is to be able to be on top of all your work all the time. This can only be achieved if you are very selective about what work you take on.

3 USE A SIMPLE SYSTEM

Here is a very simple time management system, which is based on the principles I've been discussing. The result is that in spite of its simplicity it's nevertheless immensely powerful. Of all the many systems I have tried out or developed myself over the last fifteen years or more, this is the one I find works best. Don't be misled by its simplicity into thinking that it is too obvious to work.

1. Write out a list of five tasks. The tasks can be any size, large or small, but you should be clear in your mind what the definition of 'finished' is with regard to each task. For larger tasks and projects you would want to define what your target is for the day, e.g. write 1,000 words of the book, list potential clients for the new initiative, clear backlog to end-July.
2. Do the tasks in order. You don't have to finish a task – just do some work on it.
3. If you finish a task, cross it off the list.
4. If you work on a task but don't finish it, cross it off the list and re-enter it at the end of the list.
5. Repeat this process until you have only two tasks left on the list.
6. Add another three tasks and repeat steps 2 to 6.

When you start work each day throw away yesterday's list and begin a fresh one. You can also start a fresh list any time that you feel that a change in circumstances has made your current list inappropriate.

Don't feed your list from another larger list. The contents of the list should come fresh from your head. This is essential if the method is to work properly. You can use reminders for specific items you don't want to forget, but that is all.

At the end of each day your task list will show you what you have actually succeeded in achieving during the day. It's a good idea to ask yourself whether what you have done is what you would have wanted to do. Did you do the right tasks? If there were tasks you ought to have done but didn't, which tasks on the list would you have omitted to make room for them?

You can then apply the answers to these questions to what you do the following day.

Putting it all together

Let's look at why the simple system I have just described works so well.

Just as we use efficiency to put our creativity into effect, so we use our creativity to be efficient. This system makes use of two creative techniques 'questioning' and 'little and often'.

The system makes us ask ourselves many times a day 'What should I be doing?' As we've seen, asking the same question many times is a very effective technique. It goes deeper than that because the questioning is repeated day after day. It's kept anchored in reality because it never takes us away from what we are actually capable of achieving in a day. This process of continuing questioning and feed-back produces very focused action.

The system also makes use of the 'little and often' technique by encouraging us to work in small bites of action. The result is that we are combining the insights received from the questioning with the deeper thought of the maturation process and the elimination of procrastination which little and often brings.

After you've used this system for a few days, you will probably find that you are falling into a natural routine for many of the tasks you do each day. This is a good thing provided that the tasks in the routine are ones that should be done. There shouldn't be a problem with this provided that you review your day in the way I've indicated at the end of the last section.

The system also encourages one further thing – and in many ways this is the most important of all. You may have wondered why the list starts with five tasks and not more or less. The answer is that this number gives considerable impulse to one's work. The system has what I call 'drawing power'. That is to say it draws one along and keeps one moving. This is a desirable feature of a time management system which is often neglected.

A list of less than five tasks lacks some drawing power. There is a tendency to dawdle and get distracted. By contrast a list longer than five tasks tends to become stale and build up resistance. I have found by experience that starting with five and replenishing when it's down to two is just the right number to keep one moving. If you try it out, I'm sure you will experience the sense of anticipation that comes from finishing three tasks and getting them out of the way so that you can replenish the list with three new tasks.

10 GROW YOUR BRAIN

I keep the subject constantly before me, and wait till the first dawnings open slowly, by little and little, into a full and clear light.
Isaac Newton, on being asked how he made his discoveries

Thinking is the hardest work there is, which is probably the reason so few engage in it.
Henry Ford

It's not that I'm so smart; it's just that I stay with problems longer.
Albert Einstein

Your brain – every brain – is a work in progress. It is 'plastic.' From the day we're born to the day we die, it continuously revises and remodels, improving or slowly declining, as a function of how we use it.
Michael Merzenich

Repetitive activity becomes part of your character.
Elliott Thulse

For major productive work you literally need to grow your brain so that it is capable of it.

This requires serious development of systems and routines so that they become so well practised that you don't have to think about them. The more routines you develop to the stage at which you don't have to think about them, the more your time will be freed up for creative activity. There is only one way to get these routines established in your life – only one way to get your brain to adapt to them. That is repetitive activity in the form of continued practice. This results in actual changes to the brain.

To become a truly productive person, the first thing that you need to establish in your life is the ability to carry out repetitive activity. This may sound to you like a rather strange statement. Yet, if you think about it, what are the major characteristics of an unproductive person? We've looked in detail at these in Chapter 3. If you remember, they boiled down to three:

Be unsystematic

Overload yourself

Don't follow through

Two out of these three (be unsystematic and don't follow through) are directly related to failure to carry out repetitive activity consistently. This must be one of the first things that you aim at. Starting with the basic low-level systems you need to practise them until they are second nature.

The key to getting this practice under way is the thing that holds all the systems together regardless of their position in the hierarchy. This is the time management system. You can think of it as being similar to the operating system in a computer. Everything else depends upon it.

This needs to be right and it needs to be practised. Try and avoid choosing a time management system which encourages you to overload yourself (unfortunately the majority). You need one that encourages focus like the Five Task system I have just described in Chapter 9. If you practise this every day, you will have provided the antidote to all three of the characteristics of the unproductive person.

Another reason why a simple time management system like the Five Task system will help you is because once you've got used to it it's easier to use it than not to use it. This is the hallmark of all good systems as we saw in Chapter 4.

1 GET THE LOWER-LEVEL ROUTINES RIGHT

Be sure that you get your systems for dealing with such things as email right. When you start out on the path to becoming a productive person one of your priority tasks is sorting out your low-level systems. The aim is to develop them so that you no longer have to think about them. If you still find yourself thinking about a low-level system after you think that you've got it established then this is a signal that it is not yet right.

One reason it is important to get low-level systems right at an early stage is that continuous repetition of faulty actions results in engraining those faulty actions. This is why you see people continuing to do things in a non-efficient manner throughout almost an entire working career. They say that 10,000 hours of practice can turn you into a concert pianist, but what they don't say is that it can also turn you into someone whose faulty methods are set in stone.

The essential thing is to practise your low-level routines until they become second nature. For instance once you have decided what your system for dealing with email is, stick to it. Make sure it is fully carried out. If you find that some part of it isn't working use the questioning methods (Chapters 5 and 6) to put it right. Don't however just change it for the sake of changing it. You can't establish a routine in your mind if you keep chopping and changing it. Do all you can to get it right, and then practise it until you don't have to think about it any longer.

The aim is to be putting your mental effort into the content of the individual emails, not into how you are handling 'email' in general. Don't forget the two alarm words 'always' and 'never' which are the indicators of a systems failure (see Chapter 4).

Many creative people think that they are 'above' low-level routines. It's easy to sympathize with this view. If you are someone who is producing wonderful works of art, brilliant music or leading the world in technical innovation, the last thing you want to be bothered with is mundane affairs like email and letters from the taxman.

Unfortunately creative people who think like this have got hold of the wrong end of the stick. If you ignore these mundane affairs the result will be that they make their presence felt, your life becomes chaotic and your creativity suffers as a result. I have coached quite a few singers, painters, architects, and musicians whose production of art has become blocked not because their inspiration has dried up but because they spend their time in a state of stress over the chaos in the rest of their lives.

The way to 'rise above' mundane affairs is to have such slick routines and systems for dealing with them that you no longer have to think about them.

For example, a concert pianist almost by definition has very well-established routines for practising. To be able to carry these out successfully they need to have equally well-established lower level routines for dealing with all the other business of life. Seeing these routines in terms of a hierarchy, with low-level routines at the bottom and high-level routines at the top can help artistic and creative people get them in the right perspective.

2 PRACTISE QUESTIONING UNTIL IT IS SECOND NATURE

As we have seen, questioning is an essential part of creativity – one of the two pillars of productivity. Asking questions is something which young children are very good at but unfortunately it tends to get drummed out of them once they get a bit older. The education system spends more time asking *them* questions so that by the time a person is a young adult they have got out of the habit of asking questions themselves except about pure matters of fact such as 'How much does that cost?', 'What time do we have to be at the airport?' and 'What's your email address?'

Asking more creative questions (as dealt with in Chapters 5 and 6) needs to be re-established in our lives. As with any other routine it is important to make it a regular habit – ideally a daily one. The benefit of questioning is so huge that you can't afford to neglect it.

Don't just keep questioning for your professional or work life. Get into the habit of using it for all parts of your life. It's just as effective when you are on holiday or at home as when you are at work. In fact it's a very good idea to have a question about what the best questions are that you should be asking.

3 PRACTISE TAKING ACTION UNTIL IT IS SECOND NATURE AND THEN SOME

As I mentioned at the beginning of this section, what holds everything together is the time management system that you use. Whether you use the one I recommended in Chapter 9 or some other, it's vital that you have confidence in it and actually use it. Some time management systems are very complicated and have a lot of system overhead and I would advise you to avoid those since they are difficult to stick to. You can't afford to fall off the system.

The best system is the one you are going to keep to. A very good way of sabotaging yourself is to keep changing systems. Like every other system you need to keep practising it until you no longer notice it. The Five Task system I recommend is ideal for this purpose. Apart from being extremely simple to work, it is impossible to over-commit yourself with it by running up huge lists of things to do. It allows you to do what you can do in a day and no more. What's more, because of its questioning nature it will ensure that you direct your work towards what is really important for you.

I advise getting your time management system to the stage where it is second nature as your highest initial priority in the process of becoming a productive person. With that as a firm base for your productivity, you can start to advance very quickly in other areas of your work and life.

Putting it all together

The message of this section is that repetitive actions actually make changes in one's brain. By establishing systems and making them second nature you will grow your brain so that you have the capacity to turn yourself into a truly productive person.

As an exercise I'd like you to write a letter to yourself to be read in one month's time. You can write it through a website like futureme.org, which will automatically email you the message when the time is up, or you can just put it in a drawer with a reminder in your diary to read it. Whatever method is easiest for you.

The letter doesn't need to be long, but it should cover something about where you feel you are at the moment with regard to productivity, and your hopes for where you will be at the time you read the letter. Make it personal as if you really are writing to your Future Self (you are!)

The purpose of the letter is so that you can see what progress you have made, and also to remind you to keep going if you have been slipping a bit.

THE PRODUCTIVE ATTITUDE

There are certain mental attitudes that the most productive people tend to have. In this part of the book you learn what they are and how to get them.

11 FAILURE IS YOUR FRIEND

I cannot prevent the wind from blowing, but I can adjust my sails to make it work for me.
Code of the Order of Isshin-Ryu

If a man is to lose his fortune, it is a good thing if he were poor before he acquired it, for poverty requires aptitude.
Geraldine Brooks

I've come to believe that all my past failure and frustration were actually laying the foundation for the understandings that have created the new level of living I now enjoy.
Tony Robbins

You build on failure. You use it as a stepping stone. Close the door on the past. You don't try to forget the mistakes, but you don't dwell on it. You don't let it have any of your energy, or any of your time, or any of your space.
Johnny Cash

There are no secrets to success. It is the result of preparation, hard work, and learning from failure.
Colin Powell

The title of this chapter is 'Failure is your friend'. This is a double-edged title because, as in any other form of friendship, failure can be a good friend or it can be a bad friend.

A good friend is someone we learn from and who helps us grow. It refers to someone who encourages us to do our best and keeps us going. A bad friend is the type our parents warned us against – someone who leads us astray and gets us into bad habits. Someone who prevents us from even trying to do well.

Which type of friend is failure for you?

Whether failure is a good friend or a bad friend depends entirely on your own attitude towards failure.

First of all let's look at how failure can be a bad friend to you. There are two equal and opposite ways this can happen.

The first is to be so afraid of failing that you avoid putting yourself in any position where you think you might fail. You never take risks and never venture into the unknown. Yet in spite of all your attempts to avoid failing, it could be said that this restricted way of living is a failure in itself. Your life is circumscribed by your fear of failure and you spend your entire time sticking to well-worn safe paths.

The second way failure can be a bad friend to you is the opposite of the previous one. It happens when you disregard the possibility of failure. This is sometimes the result of misapplied 'positive thinking'. This manifests itself in a completely unrealistic optimism which may prevent you from taking the most elementary steps to prevent failure. This lack of realism can also happen after a string of successes when the person starts to think that they are infallible. Often it results in a hard awakening.

That is failure as a bad friend. How about failure as a good friend? Just as there are two ways in which failure can be a bad friend, so there are two ways in which it can be a good friend.

The *possibility* that you might fail should encourage you to take a realistic attitude to what you are intending to do. This entails doing proper research and preparation. You need to ensure that you guard against failure not by avoiding doing anything new but by taking sensible precautions and making sure that you are properly equipped, both mentally and physically.

The *fact* of failure, when you have actually experienced some degree of failure, should encourage you to examine your mistakes and learn from them. This is the most important way in which failure can become a positive influence in the life of a productive person. The first unavoidable step is to admit that you have failed. It may not be a failure of the entire project, but simply some part of it which wasn't as good as it should have been. *What could I/we have done better?* is an essential question for productive people to ask after any sort of endeavour.

1 DON'T BE AFRAID OF FAILURE

The biggest failure in life is to avoid ever going out of one's comfort zone because of a fear of failure. Failure is a necessary part of success. How did you learn to ride a bicycle? By repeatedly failing at it until you succeeded. How does a child learn its mother tongue? By repeatedly failing to speak 'properly'. Avoiding the possibility of failure is a way of cutting yourself off from a huge variety of learning experiences.

In adults fear of failure is closely linked with perfectionism. Both relate more to the way we want to be perceived by others and by ourselves than about the actual consequences of failing. We feel the need to be seen as perfect. To fail at something is to lose face. However understandable this attitude is, we need to get rid of it.

Many instructional courses have a special prize for 'most improved student', which is in addition to the usual awards for the best student and the like. The winner is someone who made a difficult start on the course but by sheer determination and hard work pulled themselves up to a good standard. It's often the people who win this prize who are the most highly thought of by the instructors and judges. They are the ones who have shown qualities of courage and persistence against obstacles – the very qualities which point to success in the future.

A good aim in life is to forget about being the best, but instead aim to be the 'most improved'. This is basically what productive people do. They are not put off by early difficulties but know that hard work and practice will produce the results that they want. What's more you may well surprise yourself by finding out how often in real life the 'most improved' also turns out in the end to be the best.

2 FACE UP TO THE POSSIBILITY OF FAILURE

Once you have made sure that your attitude to failure is a healthy one, then you can approach the possibility of failure in a constructive way.

What is not constructive is to take the opposite attitude to being afraid of failure by persuading yourself that you can't possibly fail. That only serves to encourage reckless behaviour and a lack of sensible precautions. Unfortunately no one is immune from this sort of thinking. In almost everyone's life there are areas in which they are quite unfoundedly optimistic about the consequences of their actions, their capabilities or perhaps just their own 'luck'. This is not helped by the culture of 'self-esteem', which encourages children to feel good about talents which they don't actually possess and which they never will possess unless they take the time and effort to acquire them.

The idea that one can't fail can strike at any time. Sometimes it affects people who don't have much experience and have little idea of what they are letting themselves in for. On the other hand it can also affect people who have had a string of successes and are beginning to think of themselves as infallible. We can see this sort of behaviour in the 'celebrity' world all the time, but it affects everyone in some way.

The productive way to face up to the possibility of failure is to take all necessary precautions against it. That means researching the situation and weighing up the possible options in a realistic manner. It means acquiring the equipment, training and skills which are needed for success. Success can't ever be one hundred per cent guaranteed, but the chances of it can be greatly increased by good preparation.

The key word in the preceding paragraph is 'realistic'. Productive people don't indulge in negative thinking or positive thinking. They use realistic thinking. Above all, productive people are realistic because it's only a realistic view of a situation that provides a reliable base for productive action.

3 LEARN FROM THE FACT OF FAILURE

When we do experience failure, we need to approach what has gone wrong in a realistic way too. If we don't examine the reasons why we have failed or are failing then we may find ourselves condemned to make the same mistakes over and over again.

Even worse is refusing to admit that we have failed in the first place and burying the evidence. This means that not only are we failing to examine what has gone wrong but that we are actually treating something that is wrong as if it were right. This is a very dangerous thing to do.

Einstein's famous definition of insanity is 'doing the same thing over and over again and expecting different results'. It's a very well known saying, but judging by the way that most people behave it is also a very ignored saying. One of the most common ways that this manifests itself is to insist that when something goes wrong the way to put it right is to do more of what is causing the problem. The place to see this writ large is in many government programmes where ideology has taken over from evidence. But to be fair the government is only acting in the same way that individuals do. We all have a tendency to get stuck in a rut, and protect our rut, regardless of whether the rut is actually a sensible way to proceed or not.

As discussed in Chapter 6, there is nothing wrong at all with falling into routines – good routines are one of the basics of the productive life. It's the content of the routines that needs examining.

If we admit that we've failed and look closely at the reasons, then we can stop doing the same thing over and over again with the same results. Then the next time we can do it differently.

Frequently it's not the whole project that has proved a failure but only some parts of it. The danger is that we use the fact that we have succeeded overall to ignore the parts which weren't as good as they should have been. It's important that, whatever the overall result, we look in detail at what has happened. It may not be a question of failing so much as not doing as well as we had hoped. But the remedy is still the same. We need to look at the reasons we didn't do well and put them right. This is an extension of what I covered in Chapter 6 about ensuring that our systems work properly to produce the desired results.

As an exercise take any small project which you have recently completed and, regardless of whether it was a success overall or not, ask yourself the question 'What could I have done better?' You can follow that up by completing the sentence 'Next time I will...' with as many endings as you can think of.

Putting it all together

We've all seen Westerns in which operators at railroad stations tap out news of the latest bank robbery over the electric telegraph using Morse code. In the nineteenth century, a vast number of operators was needed to keep the telegraph network working, and of course these operators had to be trained to reach a high degree of speed and accuracy before they qualified. During the training it was found that almost invariably students would plateau at a speed which they simply couldn't get past, no matter how much they practised. However the trainers knew exactly what the problem was. There were certain less common letters and combinations which the operator would slow down for. These weren't practised enough in the normal course of events for them to improve. The solution was to identify what these stumbling blocks were for each student, and then get the students to practise them in isolation until they were at least as fast at them as they were at the common letters. Once this levelling out had taken place students could resume increasing their overall speed.

This is exactly the same principle that you need to use when you find that you are failing or not doing as well as you would have hoped. First, you need to identify the cause of the failure or the sticking point. Then you work out how the problem can be solved or improved, and finally practise it in isolation until it no longer slows you down.

As an exercise, identify some skill that you keep having trouble with on a regular basis. Some suggestions:

You have trouble parking your car in a restricted space

Your typing speed is held up because you are slower on certain letters

You stumble over the conjugation of some common French irregular verbs

For all of these, apply the response to failure procedure. Identify where things are going wrong. Work out how it should be done. Isolate it. And then practise, practise, practise!

This sort of small-scale response to small-scale failure will stand you in good stead when faced with larger-scale failures. Essentially the process is exactly the same. Then the next time you face a similar situation you will be prepared.

Remember: self-delusion is easy, whether it's overestimating or underestimating the difficulty of the enterprise or your own abilities. Realism is more difficult because it involves spending time and energy researching, learning, practising and preparing. But it is the only way that you will learn to advance.

12 DO REAL WORK NOT BUSY WORK

Beware the barrenness of a busy life.
Socrates

Being busy does not always mean real work. The object of all work is production or accomplishment and to either of these ends there must be forethought, system, planning, intelligence, and honest purpose, as well as perspiration. Seeming to do is not doing.
Thomas A. Edison

Life is too short to be small.
Timothy Ferriss

The best preparation for good work tomorrow is to do good work today.
Elbert Hubbard

One of the very worst uses of time is to do something very well that need not be done at all.
Brian Tracy

Real work is the work that progresses our goals, visions, career. Busy work is what we do in order to avoid real work. Another way of putting it is that real work is action, while busy work is merely activity. One of the most basic distinctions to make in our lives if we wish to be productive is the difference between action and activity.

Action is what achieves our goals, moves our business and personal lives forward, expands our horizons, produces what we want out of life and actually gets the job done. It is immensely rewarding but is also very likely to be difficult and challenging.

Activity is all the things we fill our lives with in order to avoid the difficulties and challenges of taking action. Strangely enough activity often looks more like real work than real work does. By our colleagues, and even by ourselves, we are expected to conform to the image of someone hard at work – and that image involves making phone calls, working late, dealing with email, attending meetings and generally rushing around. Real work can often look lazy. If you are an executive or run your own business then productive, focused thinking must be one of the most important bits of real work that you can do – but nevertheless sitting in your office thinking looks very like bunking off.

You can be pretty sure you have fallen into the activity trap if:

- You never have time to think. (Thinking should be your number one top priority *action*)
- You work through lunch and don't have a definite finish time in the evening. (Lack of proper breaks reduces your efficiency)
- You don't have time for exercise. (Lack of exercise reduces your working efficiency and shortens your life span)
- You don't have time for a personal life. (If your personal life isn't a top priority for you, what chance is there that the rest of your priorities make any sense?)
- You never have time to do the things you really want to do. (So what is the point of all that work?)
- You are constantly doing things which anyone else could do. (You should be concentrating on the things only you can do)
- You feel overwhelmed by low-grade trivial work.

1 DO THE REAL WORK FIRST

Since busy work is a defence against having to do real work, which challenges us and takes us out of our comfort zones, the best defence against being overwhelmed by busy work is to do the most challenging work first.

Imagine that you have five tasks to accomplish this morning. We'll call them Tasks A–E. They are in order of difficulty, with Task A being difficult and challenging and Task E being easy and routine. All of them are necessary parts of your work. Which task will you do first?

As we've seen in earlier chapters, there is a strong tendency for people to follow the path of least resistance. That means that they will go for the easiest task first, which is Task E. Once Task E has been done, the path of least resistance is to do Task D which is a little bit more difficult. Next they will progress to Task C, which is getting quite a bit more difficult and which they will do with some reluctance.

They are now faced with the two most difficult Tasks A and B. It's here that they get into difficulties with the path of least resistance. The path of least resistance no longer consists of doing Tasks A and B – they are too difficult. What then is the path of least resistance here? It's to create some new tasks at the difficulty level of D and E. To do this is very easy because there are always a multitude of tasks which could be done at this level. Never mind that they are not strictly necessary. The aim is not to get real work done but to avoid having to do the difficult tasks.

In fact what is happening here is that busy work is being created. Since busy work is very easy to create there is no reason why they should ever have to get round to Tasks A and B. They can always use how busy they are as an excuse. They have been caught by the busy-work trap, or rather have caught themselves in it.

As you can see, this is very easy to fall into. How can it be avoided?

Let's see what happens if we turn this round and go for Task A, the most difficult, first. We can make this the path of least resistance by identifying a very easy first step, then another easy step to follow. After that momentum should keep you going. After finishing Task A, go for Task B. This leaves Tasks C, D and E, which are easy. But since you have already done the difficult tasks, there is no need to invent any more tasks at this level. You have just got rid of the need for busy work.

2 LET BUSY WORK FIND ITS OWN LEVEL

The above is just a theoretical illustration. How does it work out in practice?

If you are using the time management method which I recommended in Chapter 9, then make sure that your initial list of five tasks includes a good mix of levels of difficulty. Particularly be sure to include your most challenging current project. At the moment my most challenging project is writing this book. Accordingly I put it on my list at the beginning of each day and don't take it off until the end of the day. That means that I am working on it multiple times a day. If I were writing a novel, I might want to do fewer sessions and make them longer, but nevertheless I would make sure to put it on the list right at the beginning of the day, and I wouldn't take it off until I had completed my target for the day.

Doing this with your most challenging project means that you are pretty well set to keep the busy work at bay. This is for the reason we've just seen – you don't need busy work if you are already doing your most challenging work. Even if you do let some busy work through, it will act as a relaxation between sessions on the more challenging stuff, rather than as a method of avoiding them.

Busy work is often hard to distinguish from the sort of minor low-level routines that keep our lives running smoothly, so it's best to let it find its own level rather than weed it out more vigorously. But remember this will only work if you are tackling the most challenging tasks first.

A rather different problem is allowing yourself to be distracted, for instance by finding yourself surfing the internet for hours on end. I will be giving some remedies against this in the section on time boxing (Chapter 34).

3 WEED YOUR COMMITMENTS

Work doesn't come from nowhere. It comes from the commitments we have made, whether to other people or to ourselves. Therefore if we are still finding ourselves unable to get all our work done, we need to take a look at our commitments.

A basic principle which productive people bring to their commitments is: *It's better to do a few things well than a lot of things badly.*

The productive time management system (see Chapter 9) helps with this because it restricts your list to what you are actually able to do during one day. This is all that you are able to do and there is no way around it. Therefore your commitments must not exceed what you can get done using this system.

The reason I am against to-do lists and someday/maybe lists is because they are really just flights of fancy. They are lists of projects and tasks which you don't have time to do. They refer to a never-never land where you magically get time to do all this work. What's more a list is out of date as soon as you've written it. It is a list of things which at one point in time you considered you ought to do. But it is not a list of things which you think important enough to actually do.

The only way you can start to reduce a to-do list is by skimping the things which really are important for you to be doing. Your attention gets spread around a large number of tasks and commitments, none of which are getting the time they deserve. What gets done and what doesn't get done becomes more a matter of chance than of conscious decision.

This is not a good way to proceed. To be productive you need to make careful decisions about how you are going to use the actual time you have available. It's here that we meet a further important principle for productive people: *A commitment is as much about what you are not going to do as about what you are going to do.*

When you make a genuine commitment to something you are closing off all the other things which you could have done that would get in the way of that commitment. If you decide to make a commitment to a person then you are agreeing to be faithful to that person. If you decide to change jobs and become an estate agent then you are giving up all the other professions which you considered. A commitment implies that for as long as the commitment lasts you are going to clear enough space in your life to carry out that commitment.

This is important because it is very common for people to take on commitment after commitment without clearing this space. This is always a disaster because every time you take on a new commitment without clearing space for it, you are showing that you are not really committed to it. Even worse, *you are also weakening all the other commitments you have already made.*

Putting it all together

We hear complaints all the time about the hectic pace of today's life and how much work we have. The truth is that most of us work nothing like the hours which our ancestors a couple of hundred years ago would have worked (unless they were lucky enough to belong to the very small proportion of rich people) and it would have been far harder and more demanding work too.

The problem these days is not that we have more work to do but that we have far more choice. In the past most workers had no choice about what they should do most of the time. They just got on with the task at hand. The same applied to their private lives – there was a very limited number of things to do. But today is different. We are faced with a huge number of choices, both at work and in our private lives. Being forced to make so many choices is actually tiring in itself. Decision fatigue can set in. But the main problem is that it's often easier to say yes to a choice than no. The result is that we become overloaded by the 'yes' choices we have made.

As an exercise, keep a list of every task you do each day for a week (this is easy if you are using the productive time management system from Chapter 9 because each day's list will be made for you). At the end of the week examine the lists and ask yourself whether you have actually done the things which were the most important to you. If you haven't, what have you done instead that wasn't so important?

13 KNOW WHAT YOU WANT – IN OUTLINE

If you go to work on your goals, your goals will go to work on you. If you go to work on your plan, your plan will go to work on you. Whatever good things we build end up building us.
Jim Rohn

If you have built castles in the air, your work need not be lost; that is where they should be. Now put the foundations under them.
Henry David Thoreau

If you don't know what you want, you end up with a lot you don't.
Chuck Palahniuk

If you want something you've never had, you must be willing to do something you've never done before.
Thomas Jefferson

Some people want it to happen, some wish it would happen, others make it happen.
Michael Jordan

To be a productive person it is important to know what you want. But in the beginning it's not necessary to know more detail than you need in order to start work. The details will get filled in as you work on the goal. In fact, you don't want to fill in more detail than necessary because it will hamper the natural development of your perception of the goal as you work on it.

Many books on how to achieve your goals start with the wrong premise. They assume that detailed planning is the way to achieve goals. Planning is certainly important at certain stages, particularly when the efforts of a lot of different people have to be coordinated. But it isn't planning that does the work and planning on its own achieves nothing.

Even worse is the popular type of best-selling book which advises concentrating on visualizing the goal and having a positive attitude towards it. The idea is that you will then attract what you want to yourself. Now there's nothing wrong with visualizing a goal in order to motivate yourself, and you can certainly attract results to yourself by taking appropriate action. The problem lies in the attempt to make a direct link between the visualization and the attraction, leaving out all the work that is required in order to move from the one to the other. All this oversimplification succeeds in doing is to encourage passivity – the very worst way of attracting the results you want. If you do succeed in achieving anything it will be in spite of this advice, not because of it.

If you have been reading the earlier sections of this book you will already know what achieves goals. It is *sufficient, regular, focused attention*. If you give sufficient, regular, focused attention to a project then it *will* move.

At its most simple, the correct way to work on a goal, however easy or difficult, is a circular process consisting of three steps:

> Know where you are now
> Know where you want to get to
> Move in that direction

If that sounds a bit like the way a sat nav works when you are driving a car then you have got the right idea! What I'm going to concentrate on in the remainder of this chapter is the 'Know where you want to get to' part.

1 KNOW WHAT YOU WANT

When you use a sat nav to drive a car to a certain destination how much do you need to know about the destination in order to get there?

You may know quite a lot about it already. If you are going to stay in a hotel, you may have read up about it on the internet, looked at the brochure, checked its facilities, looked at the restaurant menu and perhaps booked some tours starting from it. You may even have been to the hotel before and know it quite well.

How much of this is actually relevant to finding your way there using a sat nav? Think about the answer carefully.

The answer is that none of it is relevant. All you need to get there is the address. The sat nav is not even remotely interested in knowing anything else about the hotel.

What is the equivalent of the address when we are talking about goals rather than physical destinations?

All you need is enough information to give direction to your actions in the present moment. As you move forward your goal may become more and more specific, but it shouldn't be more specific than it needs to be. Here's a simple example from everyday life of the different degrees of specificity which might apply to a goal about going out in the evening.

> I want to do something this evening
> I want to go to a restaurant this evening
> I want to go to a Chinese restaurant this evening
> I want to go to the Old Shanghai restaurant this evening

In the first instance the vague unspecific goal 'I want to do something this evening' is enough to get me moving, thinking about what I'd like to do, discussing it with my wife and so on. Once we've decided we'd like to go to a restaurant, the original goal is no longer enough to guide my actions so it needs to become the more specific goal 'I want to go to a restaurant this evening'.

In fact my initial goal can be anywhere along the spectrum of specificity. If my one desire is to go to a particular restaurant my initial goal could be 'I want to go to the Old Shanghai restaurant this evening'.

Notice that it makes a difference which goal you start out with. Suppose your final goal is 'I want to go to the Old Shanghai restaurant this evening', but it turns out that the Old Shanghai restaurant is fully booked.

If you started with the goal 'I want to do something this evening', you will go back one step and try to book a different Chinese restaurant this evening.

If you started with the goal 'I want to go to the Old Shanghai restaurant', you will book the Old Shanghai for a different evening.

Although the goal 'I want to go to the Old Shanghai restaurant this evening' appears to be identical in both cases, it in fact differs in what happens if the goal proves impossible. In one case the next step is to book a different restaurant for the same evening, while in the other the next step is to book the same restaurant for a different evening.

This is an important distinction because goals are frequently made too specific at too early a stage. This is one of the problems with SMART goals and targets. Government targets in particular are notorious for having quite unintended consequences because a target which focuses on one specificity divorces the target from the reason it was introduced in the first place.

If we remember that a goal should be only specific enough for the purpose of guiding our actions in the present, we can get a much clearer idea of what is entailed in the goal-setting process. A goal should not be static but dynamic, and should develop as we move towards it. The initial goal will be superseded and will give way to more specific ones as a result of this development.

2 KNOW WHY YOU WANT IT

I expect you have had the experience of setting a goal and finding yourself completely stuck over it long before it is completed – or sometimes even before it's been properly begun. If this happens, one remedy is to examine in detail why you want the goal.

In my coaching days, I helped quite a few people with career change. Typically a client would be very dissatisfied with their present work, but would have no idea about what else they could do. They would often suffer from feelings of being trapped by their fears and their family responsibilities so that change was impossible. This could go on for year after year with no progress beyond the initial goal of 'I want to do something else'.

One of the first things I would get them to do was take this goal seriously as it stood instead of just regarding it as a vague aspiration. The first action I advised them to take on the goal was to write out a list of exactly why they wanted to change careers.

So they'd sit down with a piece of paper, write 'Why do I want to do something else?' and list as many reasons as they could. A partial list might go something like this:

I hate working for a boss

I don't like working fixed hours

I want to feel my talents are better used

I don't like commuting

I want to earn more money

I'm stressed and unhappy

... and so on

If you look at this list – a fairly typical one – you will see that only two of the items are things which they positively want, 'I want to feel my talents are better used' and 'I want to earn more money'. All the rest are negatives – things which they don't want.

Negatives are not good motivators. Accordingly the next step is to turn each of the negatives into positives. I used to encourage them to do this by getting them to ask themselves for each statement 'If this is what I *don't* want, then what *do* I want?'

Using this question, 'I hate working for a boss' might become 'I want to be my own boss' for example. Once they'd processed their whole list in this way it might read something like this:

> I want to be my own boss
>
> I want to work flexible hours
>
> I want to feel my talents are better used
>
> I want to live and work in the same town
>
> I want to earn more money
>
> I want to feel happy and relaxed

Notice that each of these relates to one of the entries on the first list. The positive wants have been left unchanged but the negatives have been transformed into their opposites. This doesn't mean the grammatical opposite, but what the clients see as the opposite for themselves. By doing this they have begun the process of moving towards the goal. For the first time they may be beginning to get a clearer idea about the sort of work they would like to be doing – not the exact nature of the work but its setting. They can also start asking further questions, such as 'If everything else were right, would I be prepared to accept not earning more money?'

3 KNOW WHY YOU DON'T WANT IT

Any worthwhile challenging goal will take us out of our comfort zone. Therefore it is almost always going to come with a hidden baggage of reasons we *don't* want it. We may be entirely unaware of these consciously, but they will be constantly hindering our actions in pursuit of the goal.

So the next thing I used to encourage my clients to do was to identify these hidden reasons they didn't want their goal. They did this in the same way that they identified the reasons they did want their goal. They sat down with a piece of paper and asked themselves 'Why *don't* I want to do something else?' Once they'd done this, a typical list might read something like this:

I'm scared of moving

I may run out of money

I might not succeed in finding more work

I might end up with an even worse job

I might let my family down

... and so on

In this case of course all the reasons are negative – there are no positives. I asked my clients to use the same technique they had used with the first list to process negative wishes. They had to change each negative statement into a positive by asking as before 'If this is what I *don't* want, then what *do* I want?'

The result would be a list something like this:

I want to feel comfortable about moving

I want to have a reserve of money

I want to be sure of finding more work

I want to have a better job

I want my family to feel good about the change

These are important because they are the conditions which the person needs to have in place before they move. If these are now put together with the previous list of 'wants', there is a pretty clear description of what exactly it is that the client should be aiming for. It gives a solid base for further investigation and refinement instead of just the vague aspiration that they started with.

Putting it all together

As an exercise try the process I've just described with one of your 'vague goals' – something which you have often felt you might like to do sometime but have never really got round to thinking about in detail. Don't worry, I'm not going to ask you to act on the goal (unless you want to of course!).

To summarize the procedure:

Step 1: Phrase the goal in terms of 'I want to' or 'I would like to'.

Step 2: List your reasons for wanting to do it.

Step 3: Turn any negative reasons into positives

Step 4: List your reasons for not wanting to do it.

Step 5: Turn the reasons into positives.

Step 6: Consolidate the list of positive reasons and see if there are any trade-offs you can make, e.g. if this were right, would I still have to have that?

And one additional step...

Step 7: Rephrase the original goal if necessary in the light of what you have discovered in Steps 2 to 6. You may want to turn it into more than one goal.

14 OVERCOMING NEGATIVES

If there's not drama and negativity in my life, all my songs will be really wack and boring or something.
Eminem

I'm a realist. Where I come from, 'phenomenons' don't exist. I'm from a land where people make mistakes and try again, harder, faster; where negativity is not an option.
Akshay Kumar

It's impossible to work under conditions where they confused negativity with objectivity. You can't fool the fans.
Marv Albert

Quit thinking that you must halt before the barrier of inner negativity. You need not. You can crash through... whenever we see a negative state, that is where we can destroy it.
Vernon Howard

Seeing the glass as half empty is more positive than seeing it as half full. Through such a lens the only choice is to pour more. That is righteous pessimism.
Criss Jami

A lot of confusion is caused by those proponents of 'positive thinking' who insist that it's imperative to take a positive attitude to everything and that one mustn't have negative thoughts about anything.

Yes, it is important to have a positive attitude but this needs to be grounded in reality. Alarm bells should always go off when insistence on a positive attitude is seen to be taking people away from the reality of a situation. Denying negative information is not being positive – it is being in denial. An authentically positive attitude welcomes negative information and uses it.

Contrary to popular belief productive people are just as interested in negatives as they are in positives. This is because they want to improve. Being confirmed in where they are at present is not of any great interest to them.

The way to overcome negatives is to confront them head on, take appropriate action, and practise so that they become positives. If you do nothing more than make positive affirmations or the like you are missing out the part that actually makes the difference.

1 WHEN YOU GET A NEGATIVE FEELING, TURN IT INTO A POSITIVE

In the same way that *failure is your friend* (the title of Chapter 11), negative feelings can be good friends or bad friends depending what attitude you take towards them. If you see a negative emotion as useful feedback and a pointer to the action you should be taking, then it will indeed be a good friend to you.

What negative feelings does the productive person find particularly helpful?

Fear and panic

The productive person takes fearful and panicky feelings as a spur to action. I've forgotten who said 'The best remedy for fear is action', but I have found it to be true all my life. The times when fear has really got on top of me have been when I've allowed it to paralyse me to the extent that I've avoided taking action. Once I've started to take action I've invariably found that the fear diminishes. Procrastination is often caused by fear so the best cure for procrastination is to get oneself moving, however slowly and however cautiously at first.

Envy

Envy of another person's abilities is another spur to action for productive people. Rather than wallow in the negative emotion, they take the other person's abilities as a target they can aspire to themselves. To do that the abilities don't necessarily have to be in the same field. When we see exceptional ability in any field we can be inspired to excel in our own field.

Another way in which the productive person can use the emotion positively is to seek guidance from the person who is inspiring them. It's surprising how often people who are successful are willing to share their methods and experiences with other people if they sense that they are genuinely interested in improving their own performance.

Disappointment

One of the many problems with positive thinking is that when things don't work out the way one has persuaded oneself that they must, one gets let down with a huge bump. Not only have the expected results failed to materialize but also one's whole philosophy of success has failed. A lot of people never recover from this sort of disappointment and become cynical and disillusioned. Others continue in a state of increasing unreality, imagining that they didn't succeed because they weren't positive enough. The real reason that they failed of course is that they didn't apply sufficient consistent focused attention to the project, though there are no magical guarantees that any course of action will automatically lead to success.

The productive person deals with failure and disappointment in the ways outlined in Chapter 11. They are not afraid of failure; they face up to the possibility of failure; and they learn from the fact of failure.

2 SEEK OUT CONSTRUCTIVE CRITICISM RATHER THAN PRAISE

People have always had problems receiving both criticism and praise. Excessive praise can cause the person to start cutting corners, thinking that praise is their due and that they are entitled to it. This sort of attitude is not helped by the dogmatic insistence on raising people's 'self-esteem'. Self-esteem is actually gained through the process of increasing and becoming increasingly confident in one's abilities, accomplishments and achievements. Indiscriminate praise merely encourages people to live in unreality.

Criticism is more obviously a problem. Although praise usually comes with good intentions, even if misguided, criticism can be motivated by spite, jealousy or the desire to prove that the criticizer is better than the other person. If the person criticized then responds angrily, also trying to prove that they are better than the criticizer, it's likely to degenerate into an all-out slanging match. This can easily be seen on the internet where the norms of social behaviour don't apply to the same extent as in real life.

Productive people don't particularly encourage praise, though they appreciate it when it is genuine, but they do encourage feedback, whether positive or negative. However they don't accept criticism blindly any more than they accept praise blindly. Both need to be evaluated. Some criticism is badly motivated, some is unfounded, some is due to ignorance or misunderstanding. These need to be weeded out before taking aboard the genuine points which need to be addressed.

Accordingly the process is:

> Evaluate criticism
> Go to work on the valid points

3 THE CRUCIAL QUESTION

Your progress in any project will not be based on how positive you feel or how high your self-esteem is. It will be based on your answer to the following question:

How much consistent, regular, focused attention have you brought to this?

Be clear though that focused attention is not just a question of spending a lot of time on a project. The attention must be focused.

Let's take the example of a small business owner. When starting up a small business the owner frequently is the person who does most of the work. Sometimes at the beginning it's a one-man or one-woman band. As the business starts to become successful and expand, so the owner starts to take more staff on. There are more clients, more work, and the owner has difficulty finding time to do everything that needs doing. They are working full-time on keeping the business going.

Does this mean that they are bringing focused attention to their business?

Not if they have forgotten that the job of a business's owner is to decide on the business's strategy. No one else can make those decisions. If the owner is so submerged in the day-to-day details of the business that they have no time left to think about the direction the business should be taking, then they are failing to bring focused attention to it.

In Chapter 24 I will be discussing 'the work only you can do'. In the case of this business's owner strategy is the work only they can do. In just about every type of job, there is work only you can do and it is essential that it is the prime recipient of consistent, regular, focused attention.

Putting it all together

We have seen that a productive person sees failure, negative feelings and negative criticism as signposts towards growth. As Rudyard Kipling in his poem 'If' said:

If you can meet with Triumph and Disaster
And treat those two impostors just the same...

The right attitude towards the negative is something which few people have and which can put the productive person way out in front of people who either don't face up to things which have gone wrong or get completely thrown by them.

As an exercise, think back on a situation in which you received some negative criticism to which you reacted badly. Try now to evaluate it dispassionately in the way a productive person would. The key question to ask is 'What does the person giving this criticism want me to do in future?' Then ask yourself 'Would doing this actually result in a worthwhile improvement?' Looking at the criticism in this way takes a lot of the heat out of the criticism and makes it much easier to evaluate it rationally.

15 GO FOR THE ESSENTIALS

You don't understand something until you think it's obvious.
Matthew Eric Bassett

Motherhood has a very humanizing effect. Everything gets reduced to essentials.
Meryl Streep

The three great essentials to achieve anything worthwhile are: Hard work, Stick-to-itiveness, and Common sense.
Thomas A. Edison

I went to the woods because I wished to live deliberately, to front only the essential facts of life, and see if I could not learn what it had to teach, and not, when I came to die, discover that I had not lived.
Henry David Thoreau

I do not think that there is any other quality so essential to success of any kind as the quality of perseverance. It overcomes almost everything, even nature.
John D. Rockefeller

We all say that we have far too much to do. But if you look deeper into it, you will discover the terrible secret that you are the person who has given you most of it. Even at work, it's worth asking how many things your boss is making you do and how many things you have let yourself in for of your own accord.

I've already mentioned in Chapter 9 how protective people can be about their workload. They may complain all the time about how much work they have to do, yet cannot be persuaded to take even the most obvious steps to reduce their workload.

I often used to have people come to me for coaching who said that their problem was that they had far too much to do. I soon discovered that what they wanted from me wasn't to learn how to reduce their workload but how to do even more than they were already doing.

A further problem I found with teaching time management was that after I had shown people how to get their work done more efficiently and in less time they'd use the improvement to cram even more commitments into their lives. The result was that after a short time of improvement they would end up back where they started but with a bigger and better overwhelm. So they remained hopelessly overcommitted and unable to catch up with their work. It was as if they had a need to have a certain degree of overwhelm in their lives.

The human mind has a natural tendency to expand work. If I asked you to walk round your house or your office and write down a hundred tasks that needed doing you probably wouldn't find it that difficult. The fact is that there is always an unlimited number of things you could do.

What you don't have is unlimited time to do them in. In fact you are already filling 24 hours a day with activity of some sort. If you take on new work then something in your existing activity will have to change.

This is the main reason why I advise against keeping a to-do list or a someday/maybe list. They tend to become repositories for things we could do, rather than things we are committed to doing. The only way we can actually do them is to reduce the time we spend on our existing commitments.

The things we are committed to doing are the things that we should be focusing on. If we have decided on our commitments correctly (see Chapter 3) then the time it would take to do them properly should match the time available to do them. Anything which is not part of our commitments should not have time allocated to it.

1 DISCOVER WHAT IS ESSENTIAL

Imagine that for some reason your working week has been
reduced by half indefinitely.

Of your present work load what would you continue to do?
What would you get rid of?

Answering these two questions is a good way of identifying what
is really essential about your work and what is of only secondary
importance. Now ask yourself a further question:

If you got rid of the secondary things which you've just identified
and just concentrated on the essentials right now, what difference
would giving the essentials twice the time make?

So for instance:

> If you were an author and got rid of enough
> responsibilities to be able to give twice the time to your
> writing how much difference would that make?
>
> If you were a small business owner and took on staff to
> cover most of your routine work, what difference would
> giving twice the time to planning and strategizing make?
>
> Even if you did nothing more than get rid of
> interruptions and distractions, what difference would the
> extra time make to your essential work?

2 TAKE FIXED BREAKS

A practical way of reducing the time available so you can be
more concentrated on the essentials is to take fixed breaks during
the working day. To do this, you need to introduce a rule that
during your working hours you do nothing but work, and during
breaks you do anything except work. You can institute this rule
for the chores you do at home, as well as for the work you do in
your workplace.

It's best to introduce these fixed breaks in stages. I give a detailed example of how you might do this in an office situation in Chapter 35.

The effect of enforcing fixed breaks may surprise you. You will almost certainly find that you succeed in getting more work done during your day, rather than less. What's more, the work will be of higher quality and will focus more on what really matters.

Why should this be? It's because the breaks concentrate the work that you are doing. If you have an indeterminate length of time to work in, you will tend to drift and get easily distracted. If you have a fixed time, you will just get on with it. To take a very simple example, imagine the difference between these two scenarios:

> Your boss says, 'I need you to write a short report about yesterday's meeting. Let me have it by lunchtime tomorrow.'
>
> Your boss says, 'I need you to write a short report about yesterday's meeting. Let me have it before I leave in twenty minutes' time.'

How long will it take you to write the report under each of these scenarios?

3 DON'T LET THE LOW-LEVEL ESSENTIALS SLIP

I'd like to remind you here that there is a hierarchy of work systems, and that the high-level systems will only work properly if the low-level systems are working properly. This means that you can't afford to let the low-level systems slip.

Beware of trying to prioritize by importance. This is a trap which many people fall into and it can cause a lot of problems because it neglects the low-level systems in favour of the higher-level ones. However the fact that systems are in a hierarchy means that the higher-level systems are dependent on the lower-level systems for their correct functioning. As a consequence of this, individual tasks cannot be prioritized by importance.

In fact importance is only really relevant when deciding whether to enter into or withdraw from a commitment. While a commitment is in force everything relating to that commitment has to be done. It has to be done to the standard and within the timescale specified in the commitment (explicitly or implicitly).

To illustrate this think of a country which enters into two treaties. One is hugely important to the country because it regulates the trade between it and the largest of its trading partners. The other treaty is merely a matter of tidying up a minor question about postal rates between it and a small insignificant state. Once the treaties have been signed they are both equally binding on the country. It has to respect the provisions of both for however long they remain in force.

It's exactly the same with your commitments. Regardless of how important they were to you when you took them on, you have to keep to their provisions for as long as they remain commitments. What that means in effect is that all your work is of equal importance. And by 'work' here I mean everything that arises out of the commitments you have made.

Low-level or high-level, it all needs to be done if it relates to a commitment. If it doesn't relate to a commitment, then you shouldn't be doing it.

Putting it all together

What is an essential? Answer: Everything that is part of your commitments.

What are your essential commitments? Answer: All the commitments you have entered into.

What makes a commitment essential? Answer: The fact that you have entered into it.

How can you reduce the number of essentials? Answer: By reducing the number of your commitments.

What is a non-essential? Answer: Anything that is not part of your commitments.

16 KEEP WHAT WORKS

Absorb what is useful, Discard what is not, Add what is uniquely your own.

Bruce Lee

Visionary companies make some of their best moves by experimentation, trial and error, opportunism, and—quite literally—accident. What looks in retrospect like brilliant foresight and preplanning was often the result of 'Let's just try a lot of stuff and keep what works.'

Jim Collins

What works good is better than what looks good, because what works good lasts.

Ray Eames

Do Something. If it works, do more of it. If it doesn't, do something else.

Franklin D. Roosevelt

The idea that new code is better than old is patently absurd. Old code has been used. It has been tested. Lots of bugs have been found, and they've been fixed. There's nothing wrong with it. It doesn't acquire bugs just by sitting around on your hard drive.

Joel Spolsky

Do you feel a sense of dread every time your favourite app goes through a major 'improvement', your bank tells you that they 'have upgraded their services', the government announces a major 'reform', or your place of work decides to 'reorganize'?

You just know that all of these 'improvements' and 'upgrades' are going to be changes for the worse. Not only will there be a host of untried new stuff which won't work properly, but also all the things that were working perfectly well already will be swept away.

It sounds obvious to say 'Keep what works', but that principle is ignored time and time again by governments, firms and organizations of all kinds. Most of the time there's nothing much that we as individual customers, citizens or employees can do about it.

What we *can* control though is whether we are observing the principle ourselves in our own lives and businesses. To do this it is essential to have clearly identified exactly what is working well. If we haven't, then we are hardly going to be in a position to be able to build on it.

1 IDENTIFY WHAT IS WORKING IN YOUR LIFE

Many books about time management and personal organization spend a lot of time drawing our attention to how to fix problems and sort out things that don't work. This is only what one would expect, but it does mean that the parts of our lives and businesses which are already working well get hardly a mention. That leaves them vulnerable to being swept aside in the general changes.

Whenever you are contemplating making changes in your life, your business or your organization, it is a good idea to start off by making a list of everything that is working well and that you don't want to change. This is best done even before you draw up your list of what is not working. Doing this helps you to avoid the common error of putting all your emphasis on change, regardless of what needs to be kept.

As an exercise, have a look at your system for keeping your office tidy. If for some reason that's not a suitable subject for the exercise, pick another comparable one. Write a list of everything about that system which works well. Once you've done that, write another list of everything about it that doesn't work well. Keep these two lists for the moment because I will give you a further exercise involving them later in this chapter.

2 BUILD ON IT

The principle of building on what works applies in just about any circumstances. For now let's look at a business context. Suppose that you run your own business and you want to expand. Following the principle of building on what works, you start off by looking first at what is working well – as I asked you to do in the last exercise with your office tidying system. To do this you may need to do some research into the sales and profits figures. It's important not to neglect this research because often the figures will tell you a different story from what you currently believe to be the case.

Once you have identified what is working, look at it closely to see how you can build on it. Building on what works is a better way of proceeding than trying to make things work which don't work.

Here I want to give you an example from my own experience. When I was running my own business, a significant part of it was giving seminars on time management. I wanted to expand the audience for these seminars and increase the income that was coming from them.

I spent quite a lot of time trying to think how I could run seminars around the country. I was concerned that it would involve a lot of work, and I thought that I might have to employ a manager to organize them. I wasn't very keen to do this for a variety of reasons, but I couldn't see any alternative.

Before finally committing myself to this path, I decided to look at what was working already. One item on the list was that I had run a few seminars in my own town very cheaply and with a minimum amount of work to organize them. Because of these factors I had made more profit than usual on these seminars.

I decided to build on this, rather than continue with my initial idea of running seminars all over the country. Accordingly I concentrated on running seminars in my home town using the same venue each time. As they were easy to organize I could run a lot of them, and as they were cheaper to run, I could cut the price. And because of the low price I could fill as many seminars as I wanted to run. The low price also meant that the attendees could afford to come to me rather than me going to them.

As I'd hoped, these seminars proved very popular. For a minimum effort I was able to run a much larger number of seminars – simply because I'd looked at what was working already. Because I was basically running the same seminar over and over again all the actions involved in running it could be turned into routines which meant I hardly had to think about them.

3 WHEN YOU FIND SOMETHING NEW THAT WORKS HOLD ON TO IT

In the seminar example I've just given, the fact that I'd decided to concentrate on seminars in my home town still left open the option of some day running bigger-ticket seminars nationwide or even internationally. If I had decided to do that at some stage, then again I would start by looking at what was already working.

What was already working was of course the cheap, frequent seminars which I had now set up in my home town. Now that I'd found this new thing that worked, I was not going to let go of it. Instead I would use it for building further.

There was in fact something else that worked. I had done quite a few seminars away from home for companies and organizations. They did all the organization, so all I basically had to do was to turn up.

This meant that I now had two ways of arranging seminars, both needing minimal organization by myself. They worked and I had every intention of holding on to them. Following the principle of building on what works, how could I have produced something new out of them? Well, what I actually did was as follows.

Whenever someone wrote to me asking if I was going to be giving a seminar in their part of the country I suggested that they themselves organized one locally. I offered them a commission on the event and free attendance for themselves. They would organize the venue and drum up attendance locally. I would also advertise the event on my own networks and between the two a good attendance could almost be guaranteed. Just like the seminars for firms and organizations, basically all I had to do was to turn up.

So now I had three types of seminar organization that worked. I intended to hold on to all three of them, but my options were still completely open for developing them further.

That is a very elementary example of how to keep what works and build on it. The point to note is that this principle works at all levels, not just at the level of an initiative by a small one-person business. As an exercise let's try something on a rather smaller scale.

Take the two lists you produced in section 1 of this chapter. If you recall, the subject is how well you keep your office tidy. One list should consist of what is working well and the other of what is not working. We are already one step ahead of the usual problem-solving method which looks only at what is not working.

First, have a quick look through the list of what is not working to remind you of the contents then put that list to one side. Then take the list of what is working and see what you can build on it. For instance, if you normally succeed in keeping your desk tidy but not your files, how can you extend the methods you use on your desk to your files as well?

There's a lot of sense in the old saying 'If it ain't broke, don't fix it'. We can save ourselves a lot of needless upheaval, effort and expense if we remember it.

How much of a slave are you to the new?

Have a look around your own electronic devices and ask yourself how old the hardware and software are and whether they work fine. Have you updated them just because you felt a need for the latest upgrade or because you really needed to?

If I try this exercise in my own office, the first thing I see is my computer which is about four years old. I've no intention of replacing it anytime in the near future. The program I most often use is Word 2007. That's an antique in computer terms, but still does everything I need it to, so I have no intention of replacing it either. My finance program is Quicken 2000, which isn't even still supported in the United Kingdom. But it does everything I need so I'm keeping it. On the other hand my browser and my copy of Evernote are kept completely up-to-date since the downloads are free. I haven't been overjoyed by some of the changes they've made, but on the whole the pluses have outweighed the minuses.

However I can't claim to have been so virtuous with my smartphone which is last year's model and which I will definitely replace as soon as my two-year contract is up. Why? Because people notice things like whether you've got the latest model. And it's shiny...

Can you do better than me?

17 JUNK WHAT DOESN'T WORK

Never try to teach a pig to sing. You waste your time and you annoy the pig.

Mark Twain

It's fine to celebrate success but it is more important to heed the lessons of failure.

Bill Gates

Some people have no idea what they're doing, and a lot of them are really good at it.

George Carlin

If I find 10,000 ways something won't work, I haven't failed. I am not discouraged, because every wrong attempt discarded is often a step forward.

Thomas Edison

It is unwise to be too sure of one's own wisdom. It is healthy to be reminded that the strongest might weaken and the wisest might err.

Mahatma Gandhi

One of the most important characteristics of productive people is they refuse to put up with what doesn't work. Unfortunately the human propensity to keep doing things the same way as one has always done them means that it's quite possible to put up with something that doesn't work for years, even an entire lifetime.

I mentioned in Chapter 10 that 10,000 hours of practice can turn you into a concert pianist, but it can also turn you into someone whose faulty methods are set in stone. So it may need a concerted and determined effort to get rid of what doesn't work.

It is worthwhile though. Systems and objects that don't work are a constant source of annoyance, and annoyance drains energy. When something goes wrong it usually requires a work-around. The cumulative total of work-arounds during a day adds up to a large amount of wasted time.

Stuff which doesn't work and which is left hanging around is in effect clutter, mental or physical.

A further problem is that your own rickety systems can adversely affect other people as well as yourself. I'm sure you have had occasions when you have had to struggle with systems belonging to other people and been appalled at how inefficient they are. They don't just waste the time of the owner of the system but they waste your time as well. But don't forget that your own rickety systems are affecting other people in exactly the same way.

Perhaps the most compelling factor is that the best use of our efforts is with things that work. Routines that work become all but invisible once they have become habitual. As a result they use far less energy. They are economical and work quickly without holding anything up.

The first step to achieving routines that work is to identify what isn't working at the moment.

1 DON'T KEEP STUFF THAT DOESN'T WORK PROPERLY

Throughout this book when I talk about 'what doesn't work' I am mainly referring to actions, routines, ways of thinking and other abstractions rather than physical objects. However the principle applies every bit as much to physical objects. A computer that doesn't work properly or isn't up to the job is just as destructive to one's productivity as a work routine that doesn't work properly.

Generally speaking it's much more obvious when your computer doesn't work than when one of your work routines doesn't. In the case of the work routine it's easier to blame the poor results on some character defect that you possess, such as being a 'disorganized person'.

In the case of a defective computer, the remedy is obvious – get the computer repaired or replaced. If you are a person who is disorganized by nature, the remedy is far from obvious. How can you possibly eradicate a deep-seated character defect like that?

If you were to put the blame in the right place, on your defective work routines rather than your supposed character defect, you would see immediately that the remedy is the same as that for the computer – repair or replace – and just as effective.

2 IF YOU CAN'T MAKE SOMETHING WORK, MAKE IT IRRELEVANT

If you have routines and systems which you can't get to work for you, then don't spend a lot of time and energy bashing your head against a brick wall trying to improve them. Instead get something which does work. This is particularly important when it's you yourself that you are blaming for the defect. As the quote at the head of the chapter says, 'Never try to teach a pig to sing'. It just takes too much time and energy to struggle against your own lack of ability in certain areas (and everyone lacks ability in some areas). You should be concentrating on developing the areas which you are good at and which you enjoy.

Let me give you an example of this from my own life. One thing I really hate doing is invoicing. I used to procrastinate endlessly over sending out invoices. No matter how many systems I invented to get myself to send out invoices on time and how much I berated myself, I consistently failed to solve the problem. This of course is quite serious because if you don't send out invoices, you don't get paid.

In the end I admitted that I was never going to be any good at sending out invoices. As soon as I'd admitted that, I gave up trying to improve my invoicing ability. Instead I used a secretarial services firm to do the invoicing for me. End of problem.

My continual lateness with invoices made me accuse myself of all sorts of failings. When I employed someone else to do the job, my invoices started to go out spot on time. Did that mean my failings had gone away? No, it meant they were now irrelevant.

That is the key. If something is a continuing problem to you, don't keep on struggling to get it right. Just make it irrelevant. This usually means finding a way to bypass the problem. If you're no good at something, find someone who is. If what you're using doesn't do the job, find something else that does.

3 DON'T WASTE TIME ON THINGS YOU ARE NO GOOD AT

It is of course a good thing to have a wide basic education in both intellectual and practical matters. Too narrow a specialization at too early a stage can mean that you have very few mental hooks on which to hang new experiences and make sense of them. A wide knowledge of a lot of things is every bit as valuable as deep knowledge of a very restricted field. In fact it's difficult to put deep knowledge into context if you don't have wide knowledge as well.

Yet however wide or deep our knowledge is, we will all end up with a different balance. In some fields we will be far more knowledgeable or skilful than others. After a certain age our knowledge and skills usually reflect our experience.

Imagine that on a range of ten subjects, the average score is 50. So someone who was exactly on the average on each subject would score as follows:

50 50 50 50 50 50 50 50 50 50

But of course no one is ever exactly average in everything. So imagine that your scores are:

35 25 55 45 70 62 49 38 57 43

You have limited amounts of time and money available for further training. Is it best to use these to bring the low scoring subjects up to scratch or to use them to develop the high scoring subjects?

What happens if you put your efforts into improving the low score of 25? There are almost certainly some good reasons for this score being so low. You may have no interest in the subject and you may have no natural ability in it. Because of these two factors your experiences so far have probably been in fields in which that subject is not greatly needed. So attempts to improve it are going to meet some pretty formidable difficulties. What's more any improvement which you do succeed in making is likely to be wasted.

On the other hand the high score of 70 probably indicates the exact opposite as far as its subject is concerned. You are interested in the subject and have a good natural ability in it. Your experiences so far will have made good use of it. This means that if you put time into improving it, the results are likely to be excellent and there is little likelihood of the improvement being wasted.

So all other things being equal it is much better to concentrate on improving what you are good at, rather than what you are not good at.

But there are some important provisos to make. You may need a minimum score in a subject you are not good at in order to study what you are good at. In that case it is of course necessary to invest the time to get the necessary score.

It's also important to remember that those skills which are part of your high-score activity must all be practised, *especially* if they are the worst ones. Remember the example of the Morse code operators in Chapter 11. It was the letters and phrases which they were worst at which needed to be practised because they were holding back their overall progress.

Putting it all together

The title of this and the previous chapter add up to some very good advice: *Keep what works and get rid of what doesn't.* In other words it is good practice to concentrate one's energies on what does work and to waste as little energy as possible on what doesn't work.

Too many people do the exact opposite, spending a lot of energy trying to fix what doesn't work, while getting rid of what does work in the process.

If your talents lie in one direction, don't spend your time on an entirely different direction. If you do, you are taking away that time from what you really enjoy and are good at. If some things which you hate doing still have to be done, then make your own lack of enthusiasm and skill for them irrelevant by getting someone who is good at it to do it.

As an exercise, take a sheet of paper and see how many things you can identify in your office and your work which don't work properly. Include everything, large and small, physical objects, systems, programmes, routines, tidiness. Try to make it a complete list – to do this you may need to come back to it several times. Then make a start on sorting some of the items out.

18 GET LOWER LEVELS UNDER CONTROL

There can be economy only where there is efficiency.
Benjamin Disraeli

All growth depends upon activity. There is no development physically or intellectually without effort, and effort means work.
Calvin Coolidge

Whenever there is a hard job to be done I assign it to a lazy man; he is sure to find an easy way of doing it.
Walter Chrysler

Efficiency is doing better what is already being done.
Peter F. Drucker

'I don't have time' is the grown-up version of 'The dog ate my homework'.
Anon

I've already written (Chapter 4) about low-level systems and how to investigate and improve them. In this chapter I want to talk in more detail about exactly what sort of systems these are and how important they are to the whole.

Most of what I said in Chapter 4 applies equally to both high-level systems and low-level systems. However high-level systems need to be built on a firm foundation of correctly functioning low-level systems. That means that to become a truly productive person you need to give priority at the outset to getting these low-level systems right.

The importance of this cannot be stressed too much. Productivity is largely a matter of systems – systems practised until they are second nature. A good analogy would be learning to drive a car. First you learn the low-level skills such as how to operate the steering wheel, brakes and gears. Then you learn the higher-level skills such as how to drive confidently and safely in traffic. Until you are able to steer, brake and change gear without having to think about them, you are not going to be able to give your attention fully to driving in traffic. In just the same way, if you are constantly being tripped up by your low-level systems for email and time management, you are not going to be able to run the systems for a high-level project confidently.

So let's start at the beginning by identifying what low-level systems we need.

1 IDENTIFY YOUR LOW-LEVEL SYSTEMS

The ordinary business of day-to-day living takes up a very large chunk out of most people's time. Therefore to leave sufficient time for creative productive work we need to make the low-level systems which handle the day-to-day stuff as efficient as possible.

The first step is to identify what day-to-day routines you are using. Once you've identified them you need to audit them. The ones that are unnecessary should be discontinued. In a work context, systems and routines which are not contributing to the running of your business or job should go. In a personal and leisure context any routines which are not contributing to your own or your family's well-being should also be removed. Unnecessary routines are nothing more than time wasters.

If you are running your own business and have routine work which takes you away from your own work as proprietor, then farm the routines out wherever possible. It makes no sense to be taking up your time doing routine work which you could pay someone to do for less money than you could bring into the business yourself if you had the time.

2 GET THE SYSTEMS RIGHT

The foundational low-level system is your time management system. If this is not right, then everything else is going to be wrong. To use a computer analogy, it acts as the operating system for your life. I've proposed a time management system in Chapter 9 which is designed for productive work, but it is by no means the only system that works.

Whatever time management system you use it ought to have the following characteristics:

Simplicity: there should be little or no system overhead.

Drawing power: it should draw you into your work and overcome procrastination and resistance.

Thoroughness: it should encourage work to completion.

Self-limiting: it should restrict you to what you can actually do in the time you have available during the course of the day. It should not result in long lists of undone work, half-done projects or backlogs. Instead it should require you to consider carefully how many commitments you are actually able to find time for.

Many well-known time management methods are not designed to have these characteristics. So it's important to select the one you are going to use very carefully. As a starting point I suggest you use the one in Chapter 9 as it has been designed with these in mind.

If you are already using a time management system then I suggest you check it against these characteristics. Don't forget to ask the most important question of all: *What results is it producing?*

These four characteristics don't relate just to time management systems but to all low-level systems. If any of your existing systems are too complicated, cause procrastination and resistance, leave work half-done or result in piles of undone work, then they need redesigning. If you are getting these results without using any systems at all, then I suggest you introduce some!

Always bear in mind that the ultimate aim of low-level systems is to remove low-level work as far as possible below the level of conscious thought.

3 PRACTISE UNTIL SECOND NATURE

You are unlikely to succeed in removing low-level work below the level of conscious thought unless you practise your low-level systems well. You probably have plenty of skills in your life already which have already reached that unconscious level – some of them, like driving a car, may be pretty complicated. If you think back you may be able to remember when you didn't know those skills, a time when driving a car, riding a bike, typing, carving a chicken, or working the controls on your mobile phone were not second nature. How did they become second nature? By practice.

In exactly the same way, the new routines and skills which you need in order to become productive, need to be practised. And just as you didn't learn to drive a car or ride a bike overnight, you need to give them enough time. Remember that the purpose of routines is not to turn you into some sort of automaton, but to free your consciousness to work at a higher level.

Freeing your consciousness to work at a higher level sounds very impressive, but all I mean by it is that once you have the basic skills of driving as second nature, then you can forget about them and concentrate on the higher-level skill of driving well in different traffic circumstances. Once you have the basic skills of a sport, then you can forget about them and concentrate on bettering your whole game. In a similar way, you can concentrate on the work you have to do once you are no longer worrying about the mechanics of your time management system or your email system.

Like the lazy man in the Walter Chrysler quote above, the first question to ask about any piece of work is 'What's the easiest way of doing this?' This applies to the developing of systems just as much as to the planning of projects.

Some people seem to think that deliberately going out of one's way to make things as easy as possible is in some sort of way immoral – as if it were virtuous to make things difficult or as if it were necessary to expend a certain amount of effort before you 'deserved' a positive result. They remind me of the people I mentioned in Chapter 9 who are incredibly protective of their workload, as if it were essential to their own self-image.

Don't think that these attitudes are uncommon. In practice most people are subject to these sort of feelings to some degree. This is why their lives are never anything like as smooth-running as they could be. You need to be on guard against these attitudes if they start showing up in your life.

Perhaps I need to make one thing clear. Looking for the easiest way to do something is not the same as taking short cuts. Short cuts are a way of piling up trouble for later, and that is never the easiest way of doing something.

What I am talking about here is the search for simplicity and mastery. That is what the productive person is aiming for, whatever their own field of activity may be.

19 SHOW UP

Eighty percent of success is showing up.
Woody Allen

Most of an award-show host's job is showing up and keeping
a cool head and soldiering through it, whether it's the Oscars
or the Hallmark Channel's 'Hero Dog Awards'.
Rob Sheffield

You get lazy, you get sad. Start givin' up. Plain and simple.
James Dashner

I've found that luck is quite predictable. If you want more
luck, take more chances. Be more active. Show up more often.
Brian Tracy

The routines of almost all famous writers, from Charles
Darwin to John Grisham, similarly emphasize specific starting
times, or number of hours worked, or words written. Such
rituals provide a structure to work in, whether or not the
feeling of motivation or inspiration happens to be present.
They let people work alongside negative or positive
emotions, instead of getting distracted by the effort of
cultivating only positive ones.
Oliver Burkeman

It's only when you keep working at something that you see
progress. Failure to show up – whether it's at your desk, at the
practice session, the audition or the networking event – is a sure
recipe for failure. And if you are letting other people down in
the process, you will quickly get a reputation as being unreliable.
Nobody wants to work with an unreliable person.

The most important part of showing up is that you show up
regardless of what results you are getting. When you start

something new it takes a long time to see the benefits. You have to be prepared to go through several stages before you begin to feel properly rewarded for what you are doing.

The initial burst

Your initial enthusiasm can carry your through the early stages of any big project. Added to that, the biggest changes happen at the beginning. If you are unfit and you start an exercise programme you can double or even quadruple your speed or strength within a few sessions. The same applies to mental effort. If you start to learn a new language, within a very short time it stops being a completely incomprehensible jumble of noise, you learn some common expressions and you start to get a feel for how it works. When you start a new business venture you have a sense of moving forward towards a brilliant future. Your hopes are high and your motivation is burning within you.

The plateau

Your initial enthusiasm starts to wear off and you are putting in a lot of effort without seeing much in return. The huge progress you made in physical fitness each day becomes a small increase each week or month. The language training seems to make hardly any progress in spite of all the effort you are putting into it. You are working like crazy on your business but not making any money. With any major endeavour, this plateau can last *for several years*.

Make no mistake – this is the time when the foundations for your future success are being laid. Unfortunately it is also the time when there is the greatest likelihood that you will begin not to show up. Sadly many people give up just as they are about to move into the next stage.

The reward

This is where you start to see the benefit of all the work you've put in. You realize that at last you are really physically fit. You can read, write and converse in your new language. Your business becomes profitable. All the work you have done during the plateau stage is now bearing fruit. But beware! This is also the point where some people start to take their success for granted and assume that they will continue to be successful without needing to show up. Don't make this mistake.

Perhaps the important point to note here is that success in many fields is inevitable if you just keep going. If you continue to train you *will* get fit. If you continue to work on your language skills, they *will* improve. Business success is not quite so inevitable of course, but nevertheless you can vastly increase your likelihood of success by keeping going. Even if your business eventually fails, you will have learnt many lessons which will stand you in good stead for the future. You won't learn any lessons by continually chopping and changing rather than showing up.

1 USE THE POWER OF ROUTINES

Oliver Burkeman's quote at the beginning of this chapter about the routines that writers use stresses how they free the writers from the necessity to rely on feelings or inspiration. For instance to write this book I am using a combination of word count – keeping close track of my daily average – and several short writing slots per day mediated by my time management system. The point is that as long as I keep to the routine, it is completely irrelevant whether I start the day feeling inspired and motivated or bored and completely out of ideas. The inspiration comes out of the writing, not the other way round.

If you were writing a book, you probably wouldn't want to use exactly the same routine that I use – but you would need to develop an effective routine of your own. Not having a routine leaves you very vulnerable to developing writer's block. This is a very common condition and once you have it, it can be almost impossible to get yourself moving again. A good routine provides protection against getting blocked.

If you do find yourself blocked, the best way to prevent it happening again is to take steps get a routine established. But before you can introduce the routine, you have to overcome the block. To do this is a matter of forcing yourself to do some work on the subject each day, however little. Even five minutes is enough initially. Once you have started to write again, you can then move on to developing and establishing a routine which will prevent you from becoming blocked once more.

Developing routines like this is not just applicable to writing. It applies to all activities that require consistent work over a long period.

Time management is really the management of routines. They are the means by which you keep showing up regardless.

2 REMEMBER WHY YOU ARE THERE

Showing up is 80 per cent of success according to Woody Allen. So what is the other 20 per cent? Well, part of it is remembering why you are showing up in the first place.

I was interested to read in the papers a few years ago that when Native Americans first started to come across Europeans they were always amazed that the Europeans were incapable of walking in a straight line across uncharted territory. A typical European would do what most of us would do in similar circumstances – they would pick a landmark in the distance and head for it.

The problem with this is that, after you've made a few detours to avoid wild animals or difficult country, by the time you reach the landmark you may be facing in a quite different direction from what you were when you started out. So when you pick the next landmark it may well be on the wrong line.

The Native Americans knew the secret – which was to line up two landmarks instead of just relying on one. When you do this you can easily correct your direction just by keeping the two landmarks aligned. When you reach the first landmark you know what the right direction is so all you have to do is to pick another landmark in line with the more distant one.

This story is a very useful pointer to how we ensure that lower-level goals remain aligned with our high-level goals in our business or personal life. If we aim for just the lower-level goal, it is easy to end up facing in the wrong direction. If we line up the lower-level goal with its higher-level goal then we are much more likely to proceed in a straight line to our desired result.

Let's take as an example the common business practice of attending networking events. Networking is often recommended for making the contacts necessary for building a small business. Some small business owners go overboard with networking. They join networking associations, attend lots of events, talk to loads of people, and may even start organizing their own events.

Then they become disillusioned because their business, far from expanding, is suffering from the amount of time they spend away from it at networking events.

What has gone wrong?

The answer is that they have only lined their actions up on one goal. They have taken on board that 'networking is good' and have therefore lined up on the networking goal:

 Networking

The result is that they have concentrated on doing more and more networking without keeping their eyes on what the purpose of the networking is supposed to be. If they had remembered that the purpose of the networking was to expand their business they would have approached the networking in a different more focused way by lining up the two goals:

 Networking —————→ Business expansion

That way, instead of just aimlessly networking, they would do such things as set themselves targets about the number of people they would talk to about their business, made sure they had a special offer available, write down contact details, agree two-way contacts and be sure to follow up the following day.

As an exercise, you might take a look at some of your own goals to see whether they are properly lined up. For instance what might the difference be between these two?

———————→ MBA

———————→ MBA ———————→ Promotion to higher management

or these two?

———————→ Joining a gym

———————→ Joining a gym ———————→ Increased energy for work

Wherever you suspect that an activity which should be supporting a higher goal is taking on a life of its own, it's a good idea to carry out this lining up exercise.

3 GET INVOLVED

Another part of Woody Allen's remaining 20 per cent of success is to increase one's influence in one's chosen field.

Imagine that you had a new interest in life, bottle-top collecting, and you decided that you wanted to become highly influential in the bottle-top collecting world. How would you go about it?

Your immediate reaction to that question might be that you should concentrate on building up your collection of bottle-tops so you have the best collection. But that wasn't actually the question. The question was how you could become 'highly influential' in the bottle-top collecting world – not quite the same thing as having a the best bottle-top collection.

Here's how I'd do it.

I'd attend every meeting of the bottle-top collecting society that I could so that my face became known as a regular attender. I'd attend as many courses and events as I could so that I got to know people.

Then when the inevitable call for someone to volunteer for a certain job came up, I'd volunteer. I would make sure that I did the job better than anyone had ever done it before. That job would then become the stepping stone to the next, more influential job. And so on.

Note two things about this:

1. I don't even need to have a bottle-top collection to do this.
2. It's essential to keep one's goals lined up as in section 2 for this to work. Otherwise you'll find that you get stuck in some dead-end time-consuming job for ten years or more.

Now I want to reassure everyone that I have no interest whatsoever in taking over the bottle-top collecting world. This is just an illustration of the basic way in which people extend their influence in any organization.

To have influence you have to be involved, and you have to keep your eye firmly on your high-level goals.

Putting it all together

Let's recap what we've examined in this chapter. First it's essential in any field to 'show up', by which I mean you need to keep working at whatever it is that you are trying to achieve. Failure to show up means failure full stop.

You must also not just show up but also be involved, otherwise you are only a spectator.

Throughout this process you must keep your ultimate goals clear in your mind so that lesser goals don't take on a life of their own.

As an exercise see if you can identify a project which you have started but on which you have made no recent progress. Ask yourself what it would take to start showing up again. Then look at the price you would have to pay in time and commitment, and make a decision whether finally to abandon the project or restart it.

20 BE CONSISTENT

When you look at people who are successful, you will find that they aren't the people who are motivated, but have consistency in their motivation.

Arsene Wenger

Small disciplines repeated with consistency every day lead to great achievements gained slowly over time.

John C. Maxwell

Motivation is what gets you started. Habit is what keeps you going.

Jim Rohn

In baseball, my theory is to strive for consistency, not to worry about the numbers. If you dwell on statistics you get shortsighted, if you aim for consistency, the numbers will be there at the end.

Tom Seaver

I believe life is constantly testing us for our level of commitment, and life's greatest rewards are reserved for those who demonstrate a never-ending commitment to act until they achieve. This level of resolve can move mountains, but it must be constant and consistent. As simplistic as this may sound, it is still the common denominator separating those who live their dreams from those who live in regret.

Anthony Robbins

In Chapter 2, I quoted from my book *Get Everything Done and Still Have Time to Play* where I say 'Consistent, regular, focused attention is the key to success'. I put forward the contention that this was the key to Vincent van Gogh's output, but I could have applied the words equally well to Sir Isaac Newton, Henry Ford, or any one of thousands of other successful, productive people.

When I speak about 'the key to success', I mean success as defined by the person concerned. For many people this will often not be framed in terms of fame and money. For the ordinary person it may just be a matter of living their life the way they want to live it. To live your life the way you want to live it above all depends on being able to trust yourself not to let yourself down.

Failure is usually the result of a lack of consistent, regular, focused attention. It stems from being inconsistent or poorly focused. On the other hand sometimes failure is the result of being consistently focused on the wrong things. Doing something consistently wrong is certainly not a recipe for success. It's important to bear this in mind because more or less everyone is consistent about some things in their lives. It's just a question of whether those things are leading in the right direction.

1 USE THE POWER OF CONSISTENT, REGULAR, FOCUSED ATTENTION

It might be a bit simplistic to say that to be successful in some endeavour all you need is to be consistent in the effort you put in to it. But it's not really that simplistic, because consistent effort is the key to progress in almost any field of activity.

Are you someone who's tried to learn a foreign language and failed? If you are, you belong to the vast majority of people in this country. As a result, do you tell yourself 'I'm no good at languages'? If you do, you are fooling yourself. The real reason you failed is not because you are no good at languages, but because you are no good at being consistent.

Exactly the same applies to learning a musical instrument, studying for a degree, writing a thesis, organizing your office, keeping fit, maintaining your ideal weight and chairing the relocation committee. All these things require consistent effort above anything else.

Carrying out a large project is not about motivation in the usual self-improvement sense of psyching yourself up. It's about making the decision to give something the amount of regular, consistent, focused attention that it needs. That also involves making the decision to stop doing things which are going to get in the way of giving the project that sort of attention.

Natural ability does of course play a part, but what really counts is the quality of your attention. Consistent attention will beat natural ability any day, all other things being equal – but when they work together you have an unbeatable combination.

Your attention must be focused – it's no use messing around in an aimless way. It must be regular – doing something sporadically is little use. Finally it must be sufficient. A big project requires a lot of work. If you can't give it the right amount of attention, then it would be better not to take it on at all. You would just be wasting valuable time which would be better given to something else.

If you give sufficient consistent, regular, focused attention to something it *will* change.

2 HAVE AN AUTHORIZED LIST OF COMMITMENTS

Most people have a strong tendency to over-commit themselves. Commitments get taken on without really considering how much time they are going to take. Space is not cleared for a new commitment – it is just lumped on top of everything else we are doing.

If we are in employment we can try blaming our bosses for giving us too much work. Yet even people who work for themselves end up over-committed – and so do retired people. The truth is that over-commitment is usually something that we have let ourselves in for.

If you're going to succeed in giving consistent, regular, focused attention to all your commitments, then you'll need first of all to identify what your current commitments are and then take action to keep the number well pruned. The easiest way to do this is to have a written list of 'authorized commitments', in much the same way that firms have lists of authorized suppliers.

If a task doesn't relate to something on the list, then you don't do it. When you want to add a new commitment to the list, then you will need to work out how the necessary time is going to be found –usually by removing one or more of the commitments already on the list.

We must always bear in mind that there is no hidden store of time – we get exactly the same amount of time each day, day in day out. It is always an inescapable fact that if your commitments total more than 24 hours a day (including the commitment to get enough sleep and relaxation) then it will be impossible for you to do them all properly.

What happens if you don't take steps to reduce over-commitment? Only one thing can happen. Some or all of your commitments will not get the amount of attention that they need. But if you are not going to give enough attention to a commitment, what is the point of taking it on? You cannot produce consistently good results if you have more work than you have time to do.

3 WORK OUT THE TIME REQUIRED

Your best ally in the battle to reduce over-commitment is your time management system. The Productivity Time Management System which I recommended in Chapter 9 is particularly suited to helping you to get your time commitment right. The way it is constructed doesn't allow you to list more tasks than you have time to do. This means that you can examine what you have done during the course of a day and see whether what you have done is what you would have wished to do. If it is not, then it is easy to adjust.

This system naturally tends towards consistency because it makes use of the human characteristic that we tend to do much the same each day. The natural result of using the system is that we develop a routine. This is excellent news if our routine contains the right things (however we define 'right'). But it is also good news if the routine is not optimal, because the way the system is constructed makes it easy to see where we are going wrong and to change it.

We discover very quickly what we are actually capable of doing in a day. This is, sad to say, usually less than we expect. Then it is only a matter of deciding which commitments we are going to give our attention to. If we don't have time for certain commitments then it is best to face up to the fact and take the necessary action to cancel them.

Putting it all together

A commitment is about what you are not going to do as much as about what you are going to do.

To enter into a commitment you must make space for it if you are to work on it consistently. The only way to do this is to be very clear what the boundaries of your commitments are. You cannot afford to be doing stuff that isn't part of your commitments, and you also cannot afford to undergo 'commitment creep' by which your commitments gradually extend themselves until you have too many to action properly.

Your biggest weapon in the fight for consistency is your time management system. The Productivity System in Chapter 9 will show you exactly how much you are capable of doing and will prevent you from fooling yourself – something most of us are unfortunately only too prone to do.

As an exercise, take an activity which you are not doing at the moment, but which you would like to take up. Work out how long you would need to devote to it each day or each week (whichever is more appropriate). Then decide how you could fit it into your time. What would you need to stop doing to make room for it? Once you have decided this, decide whether you are prepared to take on the new commitment or not.

21 GET RID OF INTERRUPTIONS

The effectiveness of work increases according to geometric progression if there are no interruptions.
André Maurois

Being constantly the hub of a network of potential interruptions provides the excitement and importance of crisis management. As well as the false sense of efficiency in multitasking, there is the false sense of urgency in multi-interrupt processing.
Michael Foley

The average American worker has fifty interruptions a day, of which seventy percent have nothing to do with work.
W. Edwards Deming

Highly productive people know the importance of working in uninterrupted blocks of time with good focus and concentration.
Steve Pavlina

We could all give much better customer service if it weren't for the customers.
David Allen

When I was giving seminars on time management I frequently used to ask the audience, 'How many of you make a list each day of what you intend to do that day?' Usually about half the people present would put their hands up. I would then ask these people, 'And how many of you get through the whole of your list most days?' Usually only one or two people at most would put their hands up. Then I'd ask the others 'Why don't you get through your list?' And the answer would always be the same: 'Interruptions'.

At this stage I would draw their attention to a couple of things:

First, even though they had interruptions every day without fail they were still making their daily list as long as if the day were going to be interruption free.

Second, very rarely was anyone taking any systematic action to reduce the number of interruptions.

Neither of these points make much sense. Why is it that interruptions are allowed to make such inroads into so many people's working days? Interruptions seem to enjoy a sort of protected status. They cause immense disruption, but their extent and inevitability are ignored as if they were just occasional glitches instead of a daily problem for just about everyone.

I suppose part of the problem is that people think that there is nothing they can do about interruptions because they are random events. They are indeed random events but this doesn't mean that they can't be controlled. Like any other subject they can be analysed and systematized.

If we are going to analyse and systematize interruptions we can start by asking exactly what an interruption is. What is the characteristic that makes something an interruption rather than just another piece of work? It can't be that they are random events because we don't call a new customer in a shop an interruption. They would only be classed as an interruption if they tried to butt in while you were dealing with another customer. There's the clue – an interruption takes you away from something that you are already dealing with.

A working definition would therefore be 'anything which requires your immediate attention while you are dealing with something else'. The key word here is *immediate*. This points clearly to the solution, which is that the way to deal with interruptions is to reduce the degree of immediacy which they are given.

1 INTEGRATE INTERRUPTIONS WITH YOUR WORK COMMITMENTS

It's a mistake to think of interruptions as separate from your work. They are generally speaking part of your work and in some cases *are* your work. That means that the work contained in an interruption would have to be dealt with sooner or later. The trouble is caused by the fact that work that appears as an interruption is not covered by your routines – it escapes being dealt with systematically.

The people in my seminars who made out their lists without considering interruptions never included an item 'Deal with interruptions' on their daily list. If they had done so it might have encouraged them to take a more realistic attitude to interruptions. This would not just be by allowing adequate time for them – but also by starting to consider how to integrate them into normal work routines.

Since interruptions are part of your work, they are best controlled as a work subject like any other. Like any other part of your work, an individual interruption should relate to one of your commitments, and it is best dealt with as part of that commitment. This means that if you are interrupted while working on Project A by something to do with Project B and then a little later by something to do with Project C, the question is not why you are being plagued by interruptions. It is why Projects B and C are being allowed to interfere with Project A.

Putting it this way sheds new light on the source of an interruption and how to control it. The problem is no longer what to do about interruptions but how to control Project B and Project C. This then becomes a matter of drawing up adequate boundaries between projects to stop them interfering with each other.

2 DEVELOP SYSTEMS

When you cease to regard interruptions as something quite apart from your work then you can begin to incorporate them into your work systems. An interruption generally speaking only happens if you have failed to define adequately how the arrival of new work into existing projects should be handled.

To take some examples, if you have a project for 'New Clients' how do you handle calls from potential new clients? Obviously the answer to this will depend on the size and nature of your firm. But it's surprising how many small firms leave this sort of thing entirely up to chance. Or if you are a manager what sort of procedure do your subordinates have to go through in order to speak to you? An open door policy is all very well, but not at the cost of sabotaging your work.

How do you develop a system for handling interruptions? If you've been reading this book, then I hope that you are no longer a person who needs someone else to tell them how to do it. You are well on your way to being a productive person, so all you have to do is to put the principles of being productive to use. First, analyse the problem to see where the different forms of interruption are coming from. Second, analyse each type of interruption to see how it is being handled at present, and what sort of results that is producing. Third, ask questions. Fourth come up with a better system, put it in place and keep it under review.

3 REFUSE INTERRUPTIONS WHICH ARE NOT PART OF YOUR COMMITMENTS

Once you have accepted that interruptions are part of your work, then you can begin to be ruthless about any interruptions which are not part of your work. As far as possible you should not allow interruptions during your working day which do not relate to your work commitments. What do I mean by 'as far as possible'? I mean that you should never just accept that interruptions of this type are valid and should actively take steps to prevent them. Nevertheless you will probably never get rid of them entirely.

If you are working from home you are particularly vulnerable to being distracted by domestic affairs. Often a situation arises where one member of a couple works in an office some distance from home, while the other works at home. There's often an assumption that the one at home is the one who deals with domestic emergencies such as a child needing picking up from school, plus every other occurrence which needs someone to be home. To some extent this is inevitable, but if carried to excess it can lead to the one at home feeling that their work is being devalued. This is particularly the case when the partner who works at home is earning considerably more than the one who works in the office. This situation is a good example of one that should not just be accepted but should be thought through carefully together to arrive at the best solution.

Of course interruptions can also occur in non-work situations. You may have important personal projects like study, home improvement, charity committee work and so on which also need to be protected. As with work interruptions it is largely a matter of agreeing appropriate boundaries.

Putting it all together

The key to dealing with interruptions is to see that they are valid parts of your work, but that they are assuming a greater degree of immediacy than they deserve. The key therefore is to reduce the immediacy. This can be done by any number of ways.

As an exercise, identify one major type of interruption at work. Ask questions about these interruptions, such as 'Why are there so many?', 'What do they relate to?', 'What is my present system for dealing with them?', 'What boundaries could I put in place?' 'Who else is affected?' and so on.

Once you've done this exercise, you could repeat it at home. Pick some activity you are involved in – a study project would be ideal – and see how you could increase the amount of undisturbed time you have for it.

22 THROW STUFF OUT

Have nothing in your houses that you do not know to be useful, or believe to be beautiful.
William Morris

Simplicity is prerequisite for reliability.
Edsger Dijkstra

Simplicity is not the absence of clutter, that's a consequence of simplicity. Simplicity is somehow essentially describing the purpose and place of an object and product. The absence of clutter is just a clutter-free product. That's not simple.
Jonathan Ive

Don't own so much clutter that you will be relieved to see your house catch fire.
Wendell Berry

A simple life is not seeing how little we can get by with – that's poverty – but how efficiently we can put first things first...When you're clear about your purpose and your priorities, you can painlessly discard whatever does not support these, whether it's clutter in your cabinets or commitments on your calendar.
Victoria Moran

Clutter comes in many forms. Some of it is physical and some is mental. All of it drains your energies and hinders you from being truly productive. The most common types of clutter are:

1. **Physical:** I probably don't need to describe what physical clutter is since it is all too common in most people's lives. If you don't have a degree of physical clutter then you either are very organized yourself or have other people to organize things for you. For most of us fighting against clutter is a continuous

battle. Apart from looking untidy, physical clutter uses up available space and makes it difficult to find things when you need them.

2. **Backlogs:** In my time as a coach and as a time management adviser I've found that backlogs oppress people more than almost anything else. There are backlogs of tasks, backlogs of email, backlogs of filing, backlogs of just about anything. However much we try to clear them, they seem to grow inexorably.

3. **Commitments:** The worst sort of clutter is having too many commitments. This may surprise you since most people don't think of their commitments as being 'clutter'. But they share many of the same characteristics as physical clutter. Having too many commitments is draining and gets in the way of what really matters. Indeed having too many commitments usually manifests itself in physical clutter and backlogs.

By and large the solution is the same for all three forms of clutter. It's a simple solution, but that doesn't necessarily mean that it's an easy one. But if you've been waging an unceasing losing battle against clutter it's probably easier than you think it is, provided that you approach it right.

The cause of all forms of clutter is the same. *The amount of work you are processing is less than the amount of work coming in.*

There are three ways of changing this for the better, and they are best used in conjunction with each other:

1. Increase the time available.
2. Increase your efficiency.
3. Reduce the amount of work.

1 INCREASE THE TIME AVAILABLE

If you are building up clutter, the first place to look for a solution is to examine the amount of time you have available for processing work. (I dealt with this in more detail in Chapter 8.)

Identify the activities that most reduce the discretionary time available in your life. For most people in an office environment the three most common are meetings, interruptions and distractions.

I have dealt with meetings in Chapter 8 and interruptions in Chapter 21 *Get Rid of Interruptions.*

As for distractions, the best way of managing them is by building timed breaks into your working day (as described in Chapter 15). The effect of these timed breaks is to concentrate your work and stop it from drifting.

You will note that I am not advocating increasing your working hours, but instead using them more effectively. In fact, if you take what I say in Chapter 15 seriously, you may actually decrease your work time in order to work in a more concentrated fashion.

2 INCREASE YOUR EFFICIENCY

If you are not keeping up with your work and clutter is building up, then once you have finished looking at the amount of time available the next step is to examine how efficiently you are processing work.

Any activity which is not being carried out as efficiently as possible is taking up more time than it needs to – and probably it is not being done very well either. Shoddy work only serves to build up trouble for the future. When you consider the myriad activities that make up the average person's day, you can see that the disruption that can be caused by poor quality and inefficient work is enormous.

As I've said many times already in this book, efficiency is largely a matter of analysing the situation, working out a good system and then sticking to it. Although this sounds obvious, we have to face up to the fact that most people never get round to doing this.

3 REDUCE WHAT'S COMING IN

So you've reduced your meetings, interruptions and distractions to nearly zero, you have designed efficient systems for all the actions you take during the day… and you still can't prevent clutter and backlogs building up. Why?

The reason is that you've got more work than you have got time to do it. You have to reduce it.

Work doesn't come from nowhere. It comes from the commitments that you have made. That's what commitments are – promises to *do* something about something until it's done. Accordingly the way to reduce your work is not to scratch a few items off your to-do list – those are just cosmetic changes – but to carry out a serious audit of your commitments with a view to reducing them permanently. After all if you haven't got enough time to do a commitment properly, then what is the point of having it? All it is doing is reducing the effectiveness of all your other commitments.

The declutterer's motto is 'Keep what you are actually using – not what you think you might use'. The same applies to commitments. Keep the ones that you are actively taking forward and get rid of all the ones that are dying for lack of attention. If you feel that one of the dying ones is more important to you than one that you are actively taking forward – that's fine, as long as you get rid of one of them. There will be hard choices to make here, but the result of making them will be that all your remaining projects take on a new lease of life. Keep your commitments well weeded and keep only things which relate to your commitments.

Putting it all together

It is important to get your systems right *before* you undertake to get rid of clutter, whether it's physical objects, backlogs or commitments. Otherwise you will find that no sooner have you decluttered than it immediately starts building up again. These systems need to be developed and put in place for any aspect of your life that is producing clutter. They need to be sufficiently robust to prevent any reoccurrence once the decluttering process has been completed.

It's fairly obvious what sort of things systems dealing with physical objects and backlogs should entail. But what about commitments? How can you develop a system which will prevent your commitments growing again to the stage that they overtax the time you have available?

The easiest answer to this question is to make use of the self-limiting characteristics of the Productivity Time Management System (Chapter 9). When you look at what you have actually done during the day and compare it with previous days, you can see very clearly how much work you have time for. It's then your decision whether the commitments you have worked on are the right ones or not. This time management system makes it very easy to adjust what you are doing. You can continue making adjustments on a permanent basis in order to ensure that clutter, of whatever type, doesn't get in the way of what is really important to you.

23 GET IN THE FLOW

*Flow with whatever may happen and let your mind
be free. Stay centred by accepting whatever you
are doing. This is the ultimate.*
Zhuangzi

*If you are interested in something, you will focus on it, and
if you focus attention on anything, it is likely that you will
become interested in it. Many of the things we find interesting
are not so by nature, but because we took the trouble of
paying attention to them.*
Mihaly Csikszentmihalyi

*Challenges are what make life interesting, overcoming them is
what makes life meaningful.*
Joshua J. Marine

*To me, skating should look effortless even when you're doing
the hardest of elements.*
Johnny Weir

*Being at ease with not knowing is crucial for answers
to come to you.*
Eckhart Tolle

Although being productive sounds as if it is hard work, it boils
down to a series of small actions, many of which are repetitive.
When you break something down enough it ceases to be difficult.
Looked at under this sort of microscope it could be said that
everything is in fact easy.

This type of skilled action where your mastery enables you to act
at your best level of creativity is the ideal condition for reaching
a state of flow. The routines free you to pay attention to the
creative part of your work, just as expertise in the individual

skills needed to drive a car frees you to interact with the road and traffic in a holistic way.

The most noticeable characteristic of being in a flow state is that you feel that you are being carried along. This may be to the extent that it becomes more difficult to stop than to keep going.

To a great extent you will find yourself in the flow if you follow the instructions given in this section.

1 AIM TO BE CHALLENGED BUT NOT OVERWHELMED

You may remember that the characteristic I gave of real work (as opposed to busy work) is that you are challenged but not overwhelmed. If you have work which is too easy for your capabilities and knowledge then you will be bored by it. Real work gives you the opportunity to use and refine your skills and abilities, to grow and gain experience. When you are being challenged in this way, then you are very likely to enter the state of flow.

If your work is for one reason or another too challenging for you, then you will be overwhelmed and you may experience fear, stress and panic rather than flow. There are a variety of reasons why work may be too challenging, but the most common is that it requires a level of knowledge or expertise which is too high for you to be able to 'leap the gap'. Faced with this situation, many people take refuge by constructing a huge quantity of busy work as a defence.

This brings us onto another reason for work to be overwhelming, which is its sheer quantity. This is very common in situations where difficult work is being avoided. Non-challenging busy work is built up as a defence against stepping out of one's comfort zone. There is a tendency for people to prefer to be overwhelmed by the quantity of work, rather than be overwhelmed by the quality of the work required. When the quality of work is the issue it's difficult to find an excuse for non-action without admitting one's own deficiencies. Busy work on the other hand gives the illusion of doing a lot of work, even though nothing much is actually being achieved.

Another name for 'real work' is 'action', and another name for 'busy work' is 'activity'. It's easy to be involved in an endless series of activities without taking any real action. The productive person's concern is with action, not activity. If a productive person finds that they are beginning to fall into the activity trap, they will take steps to reverse this. The way this is done is by weeding out pointless activities with the aim of decreasing the volume of work. Then they will increase the challenge of the work that remains. In this way action replaces mere activity.

2 GIVE YOUR ACTIVITIES PURPOSEFUL ATTENTION

As Mihaly Csikszentmihalyi, the author of *Flow: The Psychology of Optimal Experience*, says in his quote at the beginning of this chapter, being interested in a subject works in two different directions. If you are interested in something you are likely to focus on it, but also anything you focus on is likely to become interesting for you. This is important for productive people because it means that you do not necessarily have to depend on initial enthusiasm for a subject in order to keep going. The actual process of working on it will in itself produce the interest if you allow it to.

The focused part of attention is very important. Giving something attention which is half-hearted, distracted or superficial doesn't achieve very much at all. It may be that the word 'focused' doesn't give the full meaning. Perhaps 'purposeful attention' would be a better way of indicating the sort of attention that is required. For example, skimming a book can be very purposeful, and may in fact be more effective than laboriously ploughing one's way through the book in detail. There's more about skimming in Chapter 41.

Remember that managing your attention is one of the keys to being a productive person, but you need to make sure that it is purposeful attention. Fiddling around with something in a random sort of way is not likely to lead anywhere.

3 MAKE IT REGULAR AND CONSISTENT

It's essential to bring purposeful attention as we have seen, but to make it conducive to flow you also need to make it regular and consistent. Flow works best with actions that you are familiar with. This sort of regular consistency can only be achieved by ensuring that the subject is not displaced by other projects. This underlines the importance of establishing a list of 'authorized commitments' (see Chapter 20). If you are constantly changing your emphasis from one day to the next, then you are never going to produce the sort of regular and consistent work that is necessary for productive creativity.

Putting it all together

Although being in the flow sounds rather mystical – the sort of thing that hippies were advocating in the 1960s – the best description of it is 'to be giving something regular, consistent, purposeful attention'.

This state of flow is one in which your work seems to be coming naturally, where you are riding the crest of a wave, where you feel that your abilities and talents are being used to their fullest extent. It is a state that is very easily achieved by productive people – and is quite the opposite to the sort of grinding hard work that we sometimes imagine when we think of productivity. In contrast to that, to be in the flow is to be in a state of natural creativity.

As an exercise, keep a record of what you do during one day at work. (This is easily done if you use the Productivity Time Management System.) Then examine the day's record and highlight everything that you have done which you feel has used, challenged or extended your professional skills and abilities. Another way to look at it is 'How much of this is work which only I can do?' (This is a concept which will be explored further in the next chapter.)

What you have highlighted is the *real work* which you have done during the day. Now look at the items you have not highlighted. Some of it may be busy work, some of it may need to be done but doesn't need you to do it. Ask yourself 'How can I reduce the amount of work which is not using my abilities?' Another way to look at it is 'How can I reduce the work which I am doing at present, but which doesn't need a person with my unique experience and skills to do it?'

It's too much to hope of course that any of us will entirely escape this type of work. If we work on our own in a one-person business we may have little choice about the matter. What we must do though is ensure that we do not allow our real work to be displaced by anything else.

PRODUCTIVE PROJECTS

With a productive attitude the world is your oyster. How can you make the most of it? This part of the book looks at how to ensure that you are doing the right work for you and how to carry it through.

24 THE WORK ONLY YOU CAN DO

*There is only one success – to be able to spend
your life in your own way.*
Christopher Morley

*The function of leadership is to produce more
leaders, not more followers.*
Ralph Nader

*The critical ingredient is getting off your butt and doing
something. It's as simple as that. A lot of people have ideas,
but there are few who decide to do something about them
now. Not tomorrow. Not next week. But today. The true
entrepreneur is a doer, not a dreamer.*
Nolan Bushnell

*If you just work on stuff that you like and you're passionate
about, you don't have to have a master plan with how
things will play out.*
Mark Zuckerberg

Only do what only you can do.
Paul Sloane

Whatever situation you are in there is almost invariably some
work which only you can do. No one else has the ability or
experience, or the detailed knowledge of the situation necessary.

Let's take as an example of this a small business owner –
someone who has set up a small local estate agency. We'll call her
Susan. She employs two agents, and also acts as one herself. So in
the business there are three people who are selling houses. When
business is booming all three are very busy.

So what is the work that only Susan can do? Much of the time her work appears identical to the other two agents. Yet as business owner she is the only one who can decide on policy matters, hiring and firing and the future development of the business.

The danger is that when business is booming Susan will get worked off her feet acting as an agent. The result will be that the work only she can do will get neglected. The most important part of this is the future development of the business – in other words strategizing. Rather than think deeply about where the business should be going, she will find herself too busy to think.

In this sort of situation the work only you can do must at all costs be safeguarded. If you don't do it, it doesn't get done for the simple reason that no one else is qualified to do it. Sooner or later not paying attention to this will be disastrous for the business.

1 IDENTIFY THE WORK ONLY YOU CAN DO

The concept of the work that only you can do is vital in order to focus on the right things. You have certain skills and interests which are the reason why you are in your line of work. But you also have knowledge and experience which is unique to you. If you have been any time in your job at all, there will be certain things which you know more about than any of your co-workers.

The corollary is that, if you are spending time on work which other people could do, then other people could indeed be doing it. In the example I have just given of the small firm of estate agents, Susan may find that the volume of work means that she is neglecting to take decisions she ought to be taking as owner. The remedy is to free up more time for herself by hiring more staff or distributing the work differently to the other agents.

The key equation here is whether it's going to be worth more to the business by thinking about and planning the future direction of the business or by neglecting to do this in order to concentrate on only the immediate return.

If you are a leader, entrepreneur or manager then certain decisions can only be made by you. If you are an artist, the art can only be done by you. Whatever your job, there will be certain things that depend on you and you alone because you are the expert on your own job.

2 ENSURE YOU GIVE IT SUFFICIENT ATTENTION

The work only you can do is often precisely the work that makes the difference when it comes to bringing the money in or achieving your other main aims. If you allow yourself to be distracted by other more trivial things you are not going to succeed in achieving what you want to achieve.

You are at the centre of your own life and as such you are the person who has the greatest interest in how it turns out. If you allow yourself to neglect the essential things, then why should anyone else be more interested than you are? No one else can or will take the decisions for you. You have to seize control of your own life.

It's always a good thing to remember that no one else is going to be more interested in your life or work than you are. This is especially important when you are relying on another person to do something for you. If you don't give the impression it's important to you, then why should they think it's important to them? If you fail to chase people up or don't seem worried if they miss deadlines, then they will assume it didn't really matter and go back to sleep (as far as your work is concerned anyway).

Every time you delegate something, or send an email, text or voicemail asking someone to do something, provide some information or give their permission for what you want to do, you have temporarily relinquished control of part of your project to them. You are now dependent on their reply before you can go further ahead. It is at this point that many people lose control because they don't follow up adequately.

3 DON'T SPEND TIME ON ROUTINE WORK ANYONE CAN DO

It's too much to hope that any of us will ever get to be entirely free of routine work. In fact it probably wouldn't even be desirable because our minds need the intervals of relaxation that less demanding work brings. But we do need to make sure that we have the time and opportunity to do the work only we can do. To safeguard that it's worth finding almost any way out of whatever is getting in the way. Some possible ways of reducing the load are:

Don't do it at all: If you have accumulated a lot of busy work in order to avoid doing the work that matters, then a lot of this busy work probably doesn't need to be done by anyone. Be ruthless in getting rid of anything which comes under this heading.

Pay someone else to do it: This is not always possible of course, especially if you are not in control of your own business. But to employ someone at a lower rate to do work which is preventing you from earning a higher rate is usually a good exchange.

Automate it: In this age of technology a lot of routine stuff which used to consume a lot of time can be entirely automated. For instance in my own business I entirely automated payments and bookings for coaching appointments. For a one-person business this was a real godsend. This type of automation is only too easy to do these days, and there are many other processes which can be automated.

Other ways: The three possibilities above certainly don't cover all the ways of reducing the load of routine work. If you've been reading this book you are well on your way to being a productive person, and productive people are creative. By using the creative techniques given in Chapter 6, you can think up for yourself new methods of reducing the load.

'Busy doing nothing?'

I have in the past caused some consternation by suggesting that everyone in the world is equally busy. This may sound a ridiculous thing to say, but when we talk about someone being very busy we are usually talking about what they have yet to do rather than what they have actually done. As far as what anyone has done, the fact is that we all fill 24 hours a day with *something*. If we all wrote down exactly what we'd done today, the total for each one of us would add up to 24 hours.

Some people would have longer lists of items that they had done than other people, but that would only be because the individual items were shorter in duration than those of the person who had fewer items on their list.

The question therefore is not how much got done in terms of quantity – that's the same 24 hours' worth for everyone - but what its *quality* was.

If you find that your time management system is leading you to fill your time with trivia and unimportant activities, then that's because you've put trivia and unimportant activities into your time management system. If you want your time management system to lead you to do real productive and creative work, then put things which are real productive work into your time management system.

The Productivity Time Management System which I propose in Chapter 9 highlights this question of the quality of what you are doing

25 MOVE FORWARD

Even if you fall on your face, you're still moving forward.
Victor Kiam

We keep moving forward, opening new doors, and doing new things, because we're curious and curiosity keeps leading us down new paths.
Walt Disney

Life can only be understood backwards; but it must be lived forwards.
Søren Kierkegaard

The price of inaction is far greater than the cost of making a mistake.
Meister Eckhart

Go as far as you can see; when you get there you'll be able to see farther.
Thomas Carlyle

Don't wait for opportunities to arise. It's only when you move forward that opportunities open up. If you sit around waiting for them you'll be waiting for a very long time.

Why is this? Is there some sort of magic law of attraction operating here, or what? In actual fact what is really happening here is even more fascinating than magic.

Opportunities surround us all the time, thousands of them. Most of the time we simply don't notice them because they are hidden by the huge number of things that happen to us during the average day. It's only when we start moving forward that they start to come to the forefront of our attention.

This is caused by the fact that our brains are very efficient filters of our day-to-day experience. It's just as well they are, because if they weren't we would be overwhelmed by the vast amount of data that our senses present us with. What our brains do is take all the incoming sensory information, filter it and present us with what they believe is of interest to us. This of course is putting what happens in a very simplified and non-scientific way, but it's sufficient for our purpose.

What we have to do is to convince our brains that something is indeed of real interest to us. This is not easy because our brains have a healthy scepticism towards our protestations that we intend to do something. In fact they are only convinced when we actually do something – and keep on doing it.

I'll give you an illustration of how this works from everyday life. Have you ever noticed that when you buy a new car you immediately start to notice every car of the same make and model that crosses your path? You don't have to look out for them. Your brain just produces them to you. In the same way, if you start working seriously on any activity you become aware of anything that appears in your everyday life that has a connection with it. You don't have to look out for it. It appears all ready and flagged up for your attention.

Another closely related way to produce opportunities is to keep talking about what you are doing. Talk to anyone who comes near. If you are enthusiastic about a subject, that's not difficult to do. If you do this, you will be surprised by how many contacts people have about even the most obscure subject. Back in 2000 my first book *Get Everything Done and Still Have Time to Play* was published as the result of a conversation I had with a colleague in a pub. Out of the blue she produced two contacts, both of which bore fruit. It wasn't difficult to get this to happen because my time management theories were all I ever talked about in those days!

To arrive where we want to go, all we have to do is move forward. Opportunities will arise as we do this. What do we need to keep in mind as we move forward? Let's have a look.

1 KNOW WHERE YOU WANT TO GO

The first essential thing you need in order to move forward is to know where you want to get to. I described how to approach this in Chapter 13. The point made in that chapter is that you should only define your destination in enough detail to guide your action in the present. To define it more closely may prevent the natural evolution of your action as you move forward. In the creative process the goal itself is dynamic and will change as progress is made towards it.

The business of goal-setting tends to be much too rigid in most Western teaching. We are told for instance to formulate goals in SMART format:

Specific
Measurable
Assignable
Realistic
Time-related

This is fine for use by corporate bodies, which need something specific to co-ordinate the actions of a team as part of a bigger plan. Unfortunately we also see their use advised for individual goal-setting. Personally I think this is a grave mistake. A SMART goal may be very effective for getting a team to a predetermined result, but it is not effective for encouraging creativity and initiative from individuals.

2 TAKE STEPS IN THE RIGHT DIRECTION

Now that you have decided where you are going you can start moving. You do not need a detailed plan at this stage (and may never need one). All you need to do is to start taking steps in the right direction. As soon as you start to do this you will be turning on the filter in your brain. Once you start moving in the right direction the way will open up before you. This is because the filtering effect of your brain starts to bring to your conscious attention what is relevant to your goal.

Be careful though – you have to keep moving. Once you stop moving, the filter effect of your brain will very quickly stop in response. This becomes a vicious circle. Because you've stopped moving, opportunities and ideas dry up. Because opportunities and ideas have dried up, you feel no impulse to get moving again.

If for some reason you unavoidably have to stop working on a project, then it is very important to get yourself moving on it again at the earliest opportunity. It will be much easier if you get underway again immediately than if you leave it unnecessarily long.

3 ADJUST AS YOU GO ALONG

The main reason for not having too detailed goals is because things seldom work out as planned. As a creative person your ideas will start to flow as you move forward. Opportunities will arise, as we have already seen. But also there will be setbacks – perhaps many of them – and you will need to evaluate them and adjust accordingly. All these put together mean that you cannot afford to have the straightjacket of a too rigid goal. As you move forward the goal itself will change. It may be that it will become more detailed, but it may also be that it changes in key aspects.

Your plans about how to get to the goal will also change. Just as you cannot afford to have too rigid a goal you cannot afford to have too rigid a plan. Planning is fine but should never become a rigid process that prevents you from being creative.

Putting it all together

For the productive person the actual process of obtaining a goal is very simple. You just have to keep moving in the right direction. The fact that it's simple doesn't necessarily mean that it's easy. You *will* come across obstacles and disappointments – these are part of living – but you should not let them stop you from keeping moving. This emphasis on keeping moving makes the process almost immune to changes of mood or motivation.

Do remember that the fact that you have to keep moving means that you cannot be working on too many goals at the same time. If you over-commit yourself, it's a serious matter. You will then not be able to keep moving on some of your goals – or possibly all of them – and you will lose momentum. As soon as that happens the filter in your brain will switch off and you will cease to make any further progress.

As an exercise, pick a relatively simple project that you intend to start in the near future. What I want you to do is to pay attention to how your brain filters ideas, opportunities and information concerning it. Remember the first step is to define the project in only enough detail to guide your actions in the present. The second step is to start moving in that direction. It might help to write down some notes on how the project unfolds as you move forward.

26 BE ON TOP OF YOUR WORK

Only undertake what you can do in an excellent fashion.
There are no prizes for average performance.
Brian Tracy

The guy says, 'When you work where I work, by the time you
get home, it's late. You've got to have a bite to eat, watch a
little TV, relax and get to bed. You can't sit up half the night
planning, planning, planning'. And he's the same guy who is
behind on his car payment!
Jim Rohn

Don't be afraid to give your best to what seemingly are small
jobs. Every time you conquer one it makes you that much
stronger. If you do the little jobs well, the big ones will tend to
take care of themselves.
William Patten

Just remember this: No one ever won the olive
wreath with an impressive training diary.
Marty Liquori

If you always put limits on everything you do, physical or
anything else, it will spread into your work and into your life.
There are no limits. There are only plateaus, and you must not
stay there, you must go beyond them.
Bruce Lee

What's the biggest source of energy in your life?

I would suggest that, after such staples as food, drink and
exercise, it's being on top of your work. Being on top of your
work gives you a great sense of energy and flow. Being behind
causes stress and results in exhaustion, burn-out and depression.
A simple illustration of this: think about the difference between

doing the washing up immediately after a meal and leaving it until it turns into a huge pile of dirt-encrusted dishes which you can hardly bear to look at.

Nothing is so draining as a backlog of work, or, even worse, work projects which have got completely stuck. These will all result in a generalized feeling of anxiety – a sort of black cloud hanging over you. This doesn't just affect the work that has fallen behind – it affects all your work. And not just your work but the rest of your life as well.

I used to advise clients who were suffering from work-related anxiety to go on a 'black-cloud hunt'. What they had to do was to look at the generalized feeling of anxiety and identify all the components – the things which were causing the anxiety. Then take the worst one, the biggest black cloud, and tackle it head on. What they found was that once they had removed the biggest component of their generalized anxiety they received a huge burst of energy. Often the other components just melted away almost of their own accord. And frequently after doing the thing they had been putting off for weeks or months, they said, 'What was all that about? It was easy!'

I still think the black-cloud hunt is good advice, but even better is not to get into such a position in the first place. I strongly advise adopting a 'zero inbox' approach to all your work. What this means is that you work on all your due work to completion. You keep your inbox of new email empty. You keep your inbox of new paper empty. You keep your inbox of new tasks empty. You keep your active projects fully up to date.

This is really the only way to work because each day of new tasks is followed by another day of new tasks, and if you haven't got rid of the new tasks from one day by the time you start the next day, when are you going to do them? 'When I've got more time' is the usual answer. And when exactly is that going to be?

1 ONLY UNDERTAKE WHAT YOU CAN DO IN AN EXCELLENT FASHION

If you are a productive person there is no point in wasting yourself doing sub-standard work. Brian Tracy says in the quote at the beginning of this chapter, 'There are no prizes for average performance.' Do your best at everything, and everything will reward you.

Be the person who you would want to hire for your own job. You wouldn't want to hire someone who turned out to be unreliable, always behind, uninterested in the work and who couldn't be depended on to do a first-class job.

As an exercise, write out the qualities you would be looking for if you were hiring someone to do your own work. How far do you feel that you actually fill those qualities yourself? If you think that you are lacking in some of them, use the question methods in Chapter 6 to identify what you can do about it.

2 GIVE YOUR BEST TO THE SMALL JOBS

As William Patten says in the quote at the head of this chapter, 'If you do the little jobs well the big ones will tend to take care of themselves.' This is true for two reasons. The first is that every big job is made up of smaller ones. If you do each of the jobs well that comprise the larger ones, you will have done the whole well. The second reason is that keeping on top of small jobs, even those which are not part of a bigger whole, releases energy.

Being on top of your work encourages you to be working in a flow state. Everything is just that much easier. I have stressed the importance of low-level routines so that you don't have to think about the low-level stuff. It just gets done. The more things you can provide a routine for, the freer you will be to think at a higher level.

I've mentioned already my routine for writing this book. It doesn't really matter what the routine is as long as it works. The result of having a routine is that I don't have to worry about whether the book is on time, or about getting writer's block, or how I'm going to fit the writing into the day. The routine ensures that the mechanics of getting the book written are taken care off. All I have to think about is the content – and if I keep writing that should come very easily as well.

3 DON'T LIMIT YOURSELF

Bruce Lee says in the quote at the start of this chapter, 'There are no limits.' What he is referring to is that there are no limits to the quality of what you can do. He is not suggesting that there are no limits to the amount you can do. Taking on too much is the easiest way to limit yourself. As the old saying goes, 'You can do anything, but not everything'.

Here's a very simple guide to how you can limit yourself:

> 1. Have no goals
> 2. Have more goals than you have time for
> 3. Continually change your goals

Any one of these three will effectively prevent you from being really productive. The most deadly is a combination of 2 and 3, in which you are jumping from one thing to another without concentrating on any of them for long enough to produce the intended results. Unfortunately this combination is extremely common. It leads to a fractured, stressful and adrenalin-fuelled life in which you are never on top of anything.

Productive people decide what their main priorities are, clear the decks to make time for them, and then never deviate from them. They may work extremely hard, but they have the energy that comes being on top and remaining in a state of flow. They are not de-energized by the demoralizing task of constantly trying and failing to catch up.

If you find that you can't keep up with a zero-inbox approach to your work, then you can take that as a sign that you have more work than you are capable of coping with. The solution is not to get even more stressed by expanding your efforts to catch up, but instead to take a good long look at what exactly you are trying to achieve in life and then throw out everything that isn't part of that vision.

It's always been a puzzle to me why so many people have difficulty comprehending why it is that not being able to keep up with zero inbox is a sign that you've taken on too much. They say things like 'I'd never be able to keep up with clearing everything straight away.' This is pure self-delusion. If you can't remain on top of things today, when exactly are you going to catch up? Most people say 'I'll get round to it when I have more time.' But when is this 'more time' which is mysteriously free of commitments going to manifest itself?

Remember that because of the extra speed, clarity and energy that comes from keeping on top of your work, you will actually succeed in doing *more* work than people who overload themselves – and it will be much higher quality work too.

The next chapter will deal with some productive ways of keeping your commitments to the size which you can handle.

27 KEEP YOUR COMMITMENTS WELL PRUNED

To become a big movie star like Joan Crawford, you need to wear blinders and pay single-minded attention to your career. Nobody paid attention to me, including me.
Evelyn Keyes

You've got to think about the big things while you're doing small things, so that all the small things go in the right direction.
Alvin Toffler

Not being aware of all you have to do is much like having a credit card for which you don't know the balance or the limit – it's a lot easier to be irresponsible.
David Allen

As the gardener, by severe pruning, forces the sap of the tree into one or two vigorous limbs, so should you stop off your miscellaneous activity and concentrate your force on one or a few points.
Ralph Waldo Emerson

Prune – prune businesses, products, activities, people. Do it annually.
Donald Rumsfeld

As soon as you start to displace your current work from the present into the future, you are in trouble. This is actually where people's problems with time management begin.

I gave a very simple example of this Chapter 4, where I described an email system that was designed to fail:

> Check email
>
> Ten emails have arrived
>
> Deal with five of them
>
> Leave the rest for later

Unfortunately this the way that a large proportion of people tackle their email. The outcome of this system is that five emails out of the ten received are displaced into the future. Once they have been displaced into the future they become a problem. They are uprooted from the time when they should naturally be dealt with – the present – and put into an unspecified limbo 'sometime in the future'. It wouldn't be quite so bad if they were displaced to a specific time in the future: 'I'll deal with these at 10am tomorrow morning'. But even in that case, the time that is spent dealing with emails at 10am the following day has to be subtracted from the time available to spend on all the emails that will be received that day.

This displacement of dealing with emails from the present to an unspecified future makes it difficult for people to learn to control the quantity of email they are receiving. If they were to action all emails when first received, it would become immediately obvious if they were having to spend too much time on email. They would then be forced to come to the obvious conclusion – that they need to reduce the amount of email they are receiving.

This email example unfortunately reflects how many people deal with *all* of their work. They displace it from the present where it would become obvious if they had too many commitments, and send it off into an unspecified future. If that sounds like the way that a person (or country) gets further and further into financial debt, you are understanding it right.

The way to prevent yourself getting into debt is to ensure that your expenditure does not exceed your income. The way to stay in control of your time is to ensure that your commitments do not exceed the time you have available to fulfil them. Fortunately there is an automatic way of doing this. Let's have a closer look at it.

1 USE THE PRODUCTIVITY TIME MANAGEMENT SYSTEM

The Productivity Time Management System prevents you from taking on too many commitments. It does this by not working with a to-do list at all. Instead what you get each day is a 'have done' list. This enables you to see exactly what you are capable of doing each day. The list cannot contain more than that.

When you start off with the Productivity System you will probably, like most people, have more commitments than you can fit into the time available. Because of the way the system is constructed you will find that after a few days you are working on the projects which are most important to you plus the essential daily maintenance tasks which cannot be left undone. You will then realize that you can't introduce anything else onto the list without dropping some of the things you are already doing.

This is a bit of a crunch point – because what the Productivity System has done is bring your work into the present. Here you are brought up short with the realization that you *really* can't do more than you have time for. What you can do is to make sure that the projects you deal with each day are the ones that matter.

2 MAKE SURE YOU ARE DOING THE RIGHT PROJECTS

The Productivity Time Management System will help you guard against the natural tendency of tasks and projects to increase. Whatever time management system you use, or none, this tendency is something that has to be watched carefully.

For example, you decide that you need to get fit. So you take up running since it appears to be the most effective way to become fit. You successfully get running established in your life and your fitness improves and you start to feel the benefits. So far so good.

However you have now got a taste for fitness and you decide that running on its own doesn't do enough for your upper body strength, so you decide to take up weight training as well. Again you start feeling the benefits, but you become concerned that all the running and weight training is making your body inflexible. So you start yoga classes once a week and practise daily.

Without really trying you have managed to add three major activities to your daily workload. You've probably experienced this sort of expansion in some areas of your life, whether they relate to fitness, work or leisure.

This is fine if you have made a conscious decision that this is the way you want your life to go. That entails making time for these new activities by ceasing to do other activities which are not so important to you. Remember that commitments are as much about what you are not going to do as about what you are going to do.

Unfortunately this isn't what usually happens. The new activities just get added to all the things that you are already doing. Then you wonder why it's difficult to keep to your daily exercise routine and at the same time keep up with your work and meet the various deadlines that you have. You end up working on your various projects in a haphazard and irregular way and none of them get the attention they deserve.

The Productivity Time Management System will protect you from the worst of this, but you still need to ensure that the projects you are spending time on are actually the right ones.

Before you add a new commitment to your life you need to ask yourself a few questions:

- What level am I working to? (e.g. do I just want to get fit for health reasons or do I want to win gold at the next Olympics?)
- How will this commitment effect my existing higher and lower level commitments?
- How much time do I need to spend on this per day/week?

- How good am I at estimating how long something will take? How much do I tend to underestimate by?
- Where is this time going to come from? Which existing activities am I going to stop doing in order to fit this new commitment in?

3 PRUNE REGULARLY

Whenever you find you are falling behind or neglecting some of your commitments, look at the totality of your commitments with a view to pruning them. If you are using the Productivity Time Management System or a similar system, then it's usually just a matter of checking that you are in fact doing the right things. For the purposes of pruning projects, there are two different types and they need to be handled differently:

Ongoing projects

Ongoing projects are projects that you take on a permanent or semi-permanent basis. The fitness example above of going for a run, doing weight training at the gym and practising yoga involves three ongoing projects. They each involve doing something every day, or so many times a week.

You need to strictly control the number of ongoing projects in your life, because every ongoing project you introduce permanently reduces the time you have available for other work. On the other hand, well-selected ongoing projects can have a major positive effect on your life. So it's always going to be a delicate balancing act.

Time-limited projects

Time-limited projects are projects which have a definite end. They often come with a deadline, but not always. The main characteristic of a time limited project is that it can be scheduled.

You can take advantage of this by deciding to work on a limited number of projects at one time and scheduling others to take their place on specified dates. In other words you are scheduling the major items of your work in much the same way that a company that replaces doors and windows schedules their work. If they are efficient they know how long a job is going to take and schedule appointments with the householders. They tell prospective customers exactly how long it will be before their new doors are fitted and they turn up when they say they will. An inefficient firm takes on more work than they can handle, makes vague appointments ('I may be able to get round to you on Thursday next week') and has a lot of irritated customers.

Critical to being able to accurately schedule projects in this way is the ability to estimate as accurately as possible how long a project is going to take. Most people's estimating ability is very poor, with a strong tendency to underestimate the time needed. This is particularly the case when the project isn't a regular one.

I advise against trying to schedule in this way unless your work consists of standardized units which you can easily estimate for. A better strategy is to keep all your current projects up to date, and only to take on new ones when the time becomes available.

Putting it all together

'Concentrate your force on one or a few points' said Emerson in the quote at the start of this chapter, and that advice should be the basis of all advice on how to be productive. If your attention is constantly dissipated by trying to share it among too many commitments or goals, then none of them are going to be done properly.

The Productivity Time Management System makes concentrating your work as easy as possible, because the system will match what you are doing with the time available. You will still need to make sure that what you have done is what you want to be doing. There is no getting around this, but the system makes it very easy to check.

28 THE THREE RULES OF PRIORITIZING

The key is not to prioritize what's on your schedule, but to schedule your priorities.
Stephen Covey

It's very important to prioritize. I know, for me, my family comes first. That makes every decision very easy.
Jada Pinkett Smith

Action expresses priorities.
Mahatma Gandhi

Things which matter most must never be at the mercy of things which matter least.
Johann Wolfgang von Goethe

The mark of a great man is one who knows when to set aside the important things in order to accomplish the vital ones.
Brandon Sanderson

It's always been my belief that 'prioritizing' as it is commonly understood is a mistake. It's what people engage in on their to-do lists in a vain attempt to get away from the fact that they have too much work. Almost every other time management author talks about it as if it's the solution to everything, but I remain sceptical.

Perhaps the best-known example of prioritizing is Stephen Covey's Four Quadrants. Stephen Covey had an immense amount of good stuff to say, but I don't happen to agree with the Four Quadrants. His idea was to prioritize your to-do list by putting all the tasks under four headings:

I   Urgent and Important

II Important but Not Urgent

III Urgent but Not Important

IV Not Urgent and Not Important

Covey stressed that we need to address most of our attention to Quadrant II (Important but Not Urgent), because otherwise we will find ourselves neglecting what is important in favour of what is urgent – the 'Tyranny of the Urgent' as Charles E. Hummel called it in his book of that name.

My problem is with the concept of *importance* as used in these quadrants. If something is part of your commitments then it is important by definition – because if you don't do it you are failing in one of your commitments. If a task is not part of one of your commitments, then it shouldn't be on your to-do list.

The time to decide how important something is to you is not when you are prioritizing your to-do list, but when you are deciding what commitments to take on. If everything that is part of our commitments has equal importance, then it follows that Covey's four quadrants are actually two quadrants: Urgent and Not Urgent. Prioritizing becomes a matter of urgency only. Urgency is in fact a very sensible way of prioritizing, provided of course that your commitments make sense in the first place. There are three other ways in which prioritizing can be misused. These are very common traps. Let's look at them in detail.

1 IF EVERYTHING IS TOP PRIORITY THEN NOTHING IS TOP PRIORITY

I learned over the years that when bosses say of their staff 'They need to learn to prioritize their work better', what they actually mean is 'They need to get more work done'. In other words the staff should increase the priority *of everything*.

This isn't just something that bosses say. It is something that we are quite capable of inflicting on ourselves. Our work suffers from a sort of 'priority creep', rather like certain educational results in which the suspicion was that the grades got higher and higher each year as the actual standards got lower and lower. So many students were getting A grades, that it became impossible for universities and employers to tell who actually was an outstanding student. Rather than restore the integrity of the grading system, another higher grade of A* was introduced and this of course rapidly started to go the way of the original A grade.

If people are asked to grade each of their tasks as High Priority, Normal Priority, or Low Priority for urgency, most will put a large proportion of their tasks in the High Priority category. Unfortunately that just means that most of their work has been given the same degree of urgency, which is useless for deciding what order to do things in.

The only way to make a meaningful differentiation between tasks is to put a limit on how many tasks can go in each priority. If people were asked to put not more than five tasks in the High Priority category and not more than ten in the Normal Priority category, then the grading would be of some use.

2 WHENEVER YOU INCREASE THE PRIORITY OF ONE THING, YOU DECREASE THE PRIORITY OF EVERYTHING ELSE

Imagine you have drawn up a prioritized list of 35 tasks using the High, Normal and Low categories and have restricted the number of tasks in the top two categories as recommended above. The result is that you have five High, ten Normal and twenty Low priority items. You become concerned that many items are not getting sufficient priority.

What are you going to do?

I can't speak for you of course, but what a lot of people would do is double the number of High and Normal Priority tasks.

So your spread is now ten High priority tasks, twenty Normal-priority, and five Low-priority tasks.

What has happened here? In effect you have halved the priority of each of the grades. High priority used to be the top five priority tasks, and is now the top ten. This is in fact a first-class example of grade inflation. You can still call the top grade 'High-priority' if you like but in reality it fulfils the criteria for what we used to call 'Normal priority'. If you look at it in this way you can see that what you really have now is no High-priority tasks, ten Normal-priority tasks, twenty Low-priority tasks, and five Ultra Low-priority tasks.

What you have actually done by trying to increase the priority of the items you were concerned about is to reduce the priority of everything. You have increased the problem, rather than reduced it.

This is one of the reasons why it is so unsatisfactory to use prioritizing as your main method of deciding what to do next. In the example given, when are the five items in the lowest priority going to get done? For all practical purposes the answer must be 'never' as there will always be no shortage of higher-priority stuff coming in. Yet if they are on your to-do list they must each relate to one of your commitments and therefore they need to be done.

3 THE REAL QUESTION IS NOT HOW IMPORTANT SOMETHING IS, IT'S WHETHER YOU SHOULD BE DOING IT AT ALL

Once you have added something to your list of commitments, then everything relating to that commitment needs to be done. You have committed yourself to providing work to a certain specification, and if you don't meet that specification then you have failed in your commitment. What this really means is that all tasks relating to your commitments need to be done within the timescale of the commitment. Prioritizing by importance is irrelevant – all tasks relating to your commitments have equal importance. They all need to be done.

If you find it impossible to keep up with all the tasks that relate to your commitments, then the way to solve the problem is to cut back on the number of commitments you have. You cannot solve this by trying to adjust things at the task level. If you try to do this, you will find that it results in poor performance on *all* your commitments as you juggle tasks in a battle to get on top of your work which you cannot win. Reducing your commitments on the other hand is the way to ensure that your remaining commitments will be given your full attention.

Whenever you find yourself juggling tasks, remember that it is a symptom of being overcommitted and that the solution is to cease doing certain activities altogether. Which activities you decide to give up *is* of course a matter of deciding what is most important to you.

Putting it all together

It sounds very counter-intuitive to regard all your work as being of equal importance, but it is at the basis of the 'zero-inbox' method of working. In this your priority is to clear all your work as it appears or becomes due in your life.

The only way you can keep to a 'zero-inbox' approach is by ensuring that your commitments produce no more work on average each day than you can clear on average during a day. Keeping your work in balance like this is one of the keys to productive working.

If you find that you are unable to keep your inbox at zero in all your work, that is a clear sign that you have taken on too much. As soon as you become aware of this you should take action to put it right.

One great advantage of 'zero-inbox' working is that it flags up very quickly any developing imbalance in your workload. If you do not have a 'zero-inbox' approach then you may be able to avoid facing up to the fact that you have too many commitments for a very long time.

29 DON'T DELEGATE! (NOT THE USUAL WAY ANYWAY)

You can delegate authority, but you cannot delegate responsibility.
Byron Dorgan

Leadership appears to be the art of getting others to want to do something you are convinced should be done.
Vance Packard

A leader is best when people barely know that he exists. Less good when they obey and acclaim him. Worse when they fear and despise him. Fail to honour people, and they fail to honour you. But of a good leader, when his work is done, his aim fulfilled, they will say, 'We did this ourselves'.
Lao Tzu

Everybody's got an opinion. Leaders are paid to make a decision. The difference between offering an opinion and making a decision is the difference between working for the leader and being the leader.
Bill Walsh

Nobody ever washed a rented car.
Thomas Peters

The usual way of delegating something is to dump it on someone else's desk, leave them to get on with it and then complain when they make a mess of it.

'It would have been quicker to have done it myself' is what you then find yourself saying. Well, yes, it would have been. So why didn't you do it yourself? What was the point of delegating it?

Really it was just a way of getting it off your desk and out of sight – for a while anyway.

Note the mistake you made in this sort of delegation. You gave away your responsibility for the task. Once you have given away your responsibility for a task or project to someone else you have lost control of it. This is particularly likely to happen when the task is something you don't particularly want to do or which you don't want to be bothered with. Delegating it to someone else is a way of getting rid of the whole subject only slightly superior to putting it in a drawer and hoping it will go away.

When something is delegated in this way, the person you delegate it to will sense your lack of interest, and they will tend to take their lead in this matter from you.

The truth is that if the task is part of your commitments then you cannot afford to give it less regular, focused attention than you give to any other part of your commitments. If it's not part of your commitments then you shouldn't have taken it on in the first place.

1 WHEN YOU DELEGATE, RETAIN RESPONSIBILITY

It's your project and your work. Even if it's been handed down to you by someone else, you need to make it your own. Often this can be done by re-casting the request in terms that are meaningful to you. So if your boss says, 'I want you to organize the Christmas Staff Party this year', instead of cringing and trying to think of a way to get out of it, recast it in the productive way as a question (see Chapter 5). Something like this for instance:

How can we all have a Christmas party that is really fun and that everyone will enjoy?

Putting it like this as a question makes it much easier to recruit other people to help you with the party. If you can communicate your enthusiasm to them, they will catch it and make the project their own as well. Your enthusiasm comes from the questions which you ask yourself and them.

Have a look at the difference between these two approaches:

I've been given the Christmas Staff Party to organize. I would like you to arrange the music and the decorations.

This year let's have a Christmas party that's really fun and everyone will enjoy. What sort of music and decorations do you think we should have?

Once you have recruited other people to help you, it will still be your project and your party – which you intend to enjoy too!

2 SET UP INTERMEDIATE DEADLINES

Giving people projects and then not checking on them until the projects are nearly due is a recipe for disaster. They have plenty of work of their own without having to deal with 'your' project, and it will take a corresponding place in their priorities. Asking them occasional vague questions like 'How's the music for the party coming along?' won't help much either.

You will get a vastly improved response if you set up intermediate deadlines. There are any number of reasons why intermediate deadlines improve performance. Perhaps the most important is that you are reducing the time frame in which work has to be done. It's a common enough experience that if you have a deadline a month off, then you are likely to start working on the task a few days beforehand. If you'd been given only a few days in the first place then you would have produced exactly the same result because you would have been forced to start work right away. So all the additional time is basically wasted. All it achieves is to dissipate any initial momentum that might have existed. Setting intermediate deadlines forces people to work in a shorter time frame and therefore get on with the work as quickly as possible.

An intermediate deadline is a date at which they report to you on progress so far. To use intermediate deadlines effectively, you need to:

1. Specify exactly what needs to have been done by the intermediate deadline.
2. Specify exactly how they are to report their progress back to you (meeting, email, written report, etc).
3. Remind them a few days beforehand.
4. Follow up *immediately* if they have not reported back.
5. If they have fallen behind the deadline, ask them to set a new deadline and make it clear that you expect it to be kept this time.

3 IF YOU DON'T THINK IT'S IMPORTANT, WHY SHOULD THEY?

One of the things you are aiming to establish by taking these actions is that you consider the work you are delegating to be important. After all, if *you* don't think it's important why should anyone else?

I expect most of the people reading this have had the experience of missing a deadline and then nothing happens. No one mentions it and no one follows up.

What sort of reaction does this produce in us? Very likely we query whether the deadline really mattered and, if the deadline didn't really matter, then does the action we are supposed to be taking really matter either? The result is that we still don't bother to get on with the action. We leave it undone under the theory that if someone wants it they will ask for it, and in the meantime we have plenty of other work to be getting on with.

This is exactly the way that the people *you* delegate to are going to behave. If you don't follow up, you are giving the message that you don't really care. If they get the impression you are just shuffling work off onto them which you couldn't really care less about, then the message you have given is that it's not really important. Not important to you and certainly not important to them.

Putting it all together

All that I've said applies as much to delegating sideways and even upwards as it does to delegating downwards. It applies to small acts of delegation as much as to big ones. For instance every time you send someone an email asking for a piece of information you have potentially surrendered control of that part of your work to them. If they don't reply, your work is held up until they get round to it. So even at this very basic level you should specify exactly what you want and by when. And then it is necessary to follow up quickly if they don't reply.

It is a good idea to keep a list of every email, voice message and other communication for which you are awaiting a reply. That way you can ensure that you do not lose that all-important control over what you are doing.

This also applies to the work you give to yourself. It is difficult to take deadlines you have given yourself seriously, particularly if you know that they are purely artificial ones. But the technique of getting yourself to keep to your own deadlines is exactly the same as getting other people to keep to deadlines. Once you let a deadline slip your mind will start registering it as unimportant if you don't take immediate corrective action.

If you've been given a task or project by someone who has not properly spelled out exactly what they want, you need to seize control yourself. Set your own deadline if there is no existing deadline, set intermediate deadlines if the timeframe needs them, and above all enforce the deadlines to prevent yourself from falling behind. You have to establish ownership of the delegated task in order to supply the deficiencies in the way you were tasked with it.

30 CONTINUOUS FEEDBACK

Regular feedback is one of the hardest things to drive through an organization.
Kenneth Chenault

There is a huge value in learning with instant feedback.
Anant Agarwal

We judge ourselves by what we feel capable of doing, while others judge us by what we have already done.
Henry Wadsworth Longfellow

What we think and do is limited by what we fail to notice. And when we fail to notice that we have failed to notice there's nothing we can do to change. Until we notice that failing to notice is what forms our thoughts and our deeds.
R.D. Laing

Most importantly, if you're going to ask (for feedback), be ready to change.
David Maister

Whatever activities you are engaged in – whether they include sales, advertising, learning a language, learning a musical instrument, finance, running a team, writing a book or any others of the myriad activities that people get up to – it's highly important to get feedback. If you don't get feedback you are just running blind with no idea whether your actions are having the intended effect or not.

I always remember my horror when I asked a small business owner how he kept track of his cash flow, turnover and profits, and he replied that he used the quarterly accounts. That meant that he was only getting feedback on how his firm was doing once every three months from figures that would already be at least a month out of date.

To be effective, feedback needs to be as instant as possible. This of course will vary from activity to activity. If we are practising a musical instrument or polishing up our French pronunciation then feedback can be virtually instantaneous. If we are keeping track of how we are progressing towards a goal, then feedback can be on a daily basis. Monitoring a small business's key indicators, such as cash flow and sales, can also be done on a daily basis.

The purpose of feedback is not to confirm that we have done it right, but to enable us to take corrective action. If we ignore the feedback because it isn't the way we want it to be then we are missing the entire point of it.

1 KNOW EXACTLY WHERE YOU ARE

The first basic rule about feedback is: *Before you can go anywhere you need to know where you are*. Here are some examples of how this rule applies in various work and leisure situations:

If you are in debt, you are not going to be able to start making serious inroads into the problem until you have drawn up a schedule showing exactly the extent and nature of your debts.

It's next to impossible to give your business direction until you have identified key up-to-date financial and sales indicators on which to base your decisions.

If you are having trouble with your golf swing, then getting a current assessment from a professional – preferably with a video camera – is a first step to improving it.

If you are getting behind on your thesis, then the essential minimum information is how many days there are until the deadline and how many words or chapters you still have to write.

Whatever goal you are working towards, one of the first steps is to identify where you are in relation to the goal and how you can monitor your changing position. Until you have done this you are essentially flying blind.

2 KNOW THE TRENDS

The second basic rule about feedback is: *If you don't know what direction you are going then you don't know whether you are getting nearer or further away from your destination.*

Just as essential as knowing where you are is being able to see how the picture is changing. Accordingly keep a record of your key indicators day by day (if that is the period you are working on). It helps if you can plot them visually. Being able to see your progress is immensely motivating. A graph or similar visual will alert you very quickly should the trend turn downwards.

Genuinely productive people do not work off 'a wing and a prayer'. They work from an up-to-date knowledge of what is happening in so far as it is obtainable. And that by the way means that they design it so that it *is* obtainable.

You need to beware of one thing with key indicators. They must be servants not masters. Key indicators provide feedback on how you are progressing towards your goal. They should not be confused with the goal itself. If you are writing a book, word count is a valuable indicator of whether you are on track during the writing stage. But we all know that a book is not judged by the number of its words and most of us are capable of telling when a book has been 'padded' to keep up the word count. Word count monitoring is valuable, but must never be allowed to be more than an indicator of how well you as an author are keeping to your timetable. The same caution applies to many other indicators in many other fields.

Examples of how this can go wrong are all around us. Governments and big corporations are particularly prone to fall into this trap. The indicator becomes the goal. The bed/patient ratio is adopted as an indicator of improving patient care, but it ends up with patients being turned out of hospital prematurely so as not to spoil the ratio. Testing is introduced to monitor progress in children's education, but it ends up with children's education being reduced to nothing more than how to pass the tests. Financial indicators are adopted in order to track the fundamental soundness of companies, but it ends up with companies making senseless decisions just in order to improve a financial indicator.

3 ACT ACCORDINGLY

The third basic rule about feedback is: *If you are stumbling around in the dark, then you tend to bump into things.* The converse of this rule is: *If you have enough light, then you can see where you're going.*

If you have no feedback you are the equivalent of a person stumbling around in the dark. On the other hand if you do have feedback then you can adjust your course because you can see what is happening clearly. To a large extent good feedback results in corrective action by its very nature. Just as when you are walking you naturally avoid obstacles because you can see them clearly, so feedback means that you can often adjust course without having to think about it.

Here's an example of this naturally occurring corrective action from my own experience.

I keep a daily watch on certain key indicators of my own personal finances. One of these is a cash flow forecast for my personal current account. The indicator I track is the lowest point – that is to say the point at which known future expenditure causes the bank balance to reach its lowest point before known future income causes it to rise again. I track this indicator graphically using a spreadsheet. Over the years this simple indicator has proved invaluable time and time again.

I don't just track the lowest point – I have a target for what the lowest point should be. Currently this is £5,000. Looking at the graph for the last five years, I can see that the indicator sometimes dips below this target, but quickly recovers. It also sometimes rises well above the target, but again reverts quickly back again. What I realize when I look at the graph is that I don't consciously take any corrective actions. Without really thinking about it, I tend to spend more when the indicator is above £5,000 and spend less when it's below it. Just being aware of the figures in itself influences my actions.

I'm quite happy to leave the figure where it is, but the implication is that if I wanted to I could raise my target figure to £6,000 and let the balance adjust itself accordingly. Provided the increased amount was reasonably close to the original, then my mind would probably have no problem in adjusting.

This would not work as well if I only looked at the figures on a weekly or monthly basis, and I hardly need to say that it wouldn't work at all if I didn't ever look at the figures.

Putting it all together

Continuous feedback is based on the two basic actions of productivity:

- Questioning
- Setting up systems

As such it produces changes in the way we think and act. We ask questions of the environment, of the situation and set up a system which then feeds back into our actions.

You can't have productivity without feedback. That feedback can be from yourself, from other people or from material facts. Whatever its source, it needs to be as objective as possible. Modern technology can help enormously with this. Audio and video recordings can let you see yourself in action. Websites and social media can give you near instant feedback on ideas. Computerized accounting can produces balances and other financial indicators at the touch of a button. Your phone can monitor your exercise rates. And so on. Nearly all of this would have been impossible even a few decades back.

31 SOW SEEDS

*All the flowers of tomorrow are contained in
the seeds of today.*
Chinese proverb

*Don't judge each day by the harvest you reap
but by the seeds that you plant.*
Robert Louis Stevenson

*Keep on sowing your seed, for you never know
which will grow – perhaps it all will.*
Albert Einstein

*Every problem has in it the seeds of its own solution. If you
don't have any problems, you don't get any seeds.*
Norman Vincent Peale

*The best time to sow a seed was twenty years back.
The next best time is today.*
Anon

Productive people don't sit around waiting for things to
happen to them. Nor do they go full blast into things without
preparation. The productive method is to sow seeds.

The seeds which a productive person sows are the small actions
which bear fruit in the future. They are often not so much first
steps as first ideas. They are characterized as follows:

- A seed takes only a little time to sow, therefore it can be sown
  in large quantities.

- Only a few of the seeds we sow will come to fruition, but that is enough.
- With seeds it can take a long time before anything seems to be happening. You may be reaping today what you sowed a long time ago.
- If you want things to keep happening, you need to keep sowing.

This is one of the reasons why it can take several years before a new business becomes profitable. The owners wonder why after three years of slaving away nothing seems to be happening, and then suddenly the business seems to lift off. Why has this happened? It's because of all those seeds they have been sowing for the last three years.

The reason many businesses or endeavours don't succeed is because the owners want immediate results from their actions. They don't sow the seeds that are needed for success. And they certainly don't appreciate that present success can be due to the actions one took possibly years before.

At the time, there is little or no immediate feedback to sowing seed. Therefore you have to provide your own feedback. The way to do this is to construct process goals. A process goal is about the actions you take towards a final goal, rather than the final goal itself. An example would be in the field of sales and marketing where your goal is to achieve a certain amount of sales. In order to achieve this you identify the actions which should lead to sales and construct goals for them. So you might have a goal of telephoning ten potential customers per day. As long as you achieve your ten calls a day, you have achieved your goal because you know from experience that it takes an average of twenty calls to make one sale. That means that nineteen calls will result in nothing. But those twenty calls are not wasted because you wouldn't have got the one success without them.

You can construct process goals for almost any activity. A few examples:

> Call your aunt once a month
>
> Go out for dinner once a week with your significant other
>
> Go for a run three times a week
>
> Go to bed before midnight every night
>
> Write 1,000 words of your book every day

These are the sort of actions which seem fairly insignificant on their own but over a period of time will build into solid results. In fact these solid results are all but inevitable – provided you keep on doing them.

1 KEEP TALKING ABOUT IT

I've mentioned before that one of the most effective ways of moving a project forward, particularly in the early stages, is to talk about it on every possible occasion. If you share your vision and your hopes with just about everyone you meet it's surprising how many will be able to offer concrete help as well as suggestions. They may also be able to introduce you to people who share a similar vision.

Sharing in this way also has the effect of making the project more concrete in your mind. As well as interesting and enthusing other people, you will succeed in increasing your own interest and enthusiasm. The questions other people ask you about the project will challenge you to work out the answers. Things which seemed very vague or even contradictory will quickly become more detailed and logical.

I've already told the story of how my first book got published because of a chance conversation in a pub. This chance conversation in a pub wasn't one isolated conversation. It wouldn't have happened if I hadn't been talking about the subject every chance I got.

I don't for a moment think that the identical same thing will happen to you. But if you talk about your subject on every possible occasion, what I am sure about is that *something* will happen. That something will lead to quite different results from what you would have got if you hadn't kept talking.

2 DO YOUR RESEARCH

An equally important way of sowing seeds is to research your subject. It's one thing to have a vague idea about what you would like to achieve. It's quite another to be clear and aware of what exactly is the environment in which you want to be operating. You will make a more favourable impression on the people to whom you talk about the subject if they realize that you have a realistic knowledge of what you want to do. Each bit of research leads to increased knowledge, which then attracts further research. The conversations which arise out of this research can often produce quite unexpected leads, as in my own story about getting my first book published.

Thanks to the internet, research is much easier today than it used to be in the past. One can build up a fair bit of knowledge about almost any subject without leaving one's desk. Thinking back to the days before the huge resources of the internet were available for the general public, I sometimes wonder how we managed to find out anything at all.

In fact it's not worth leaving your desk until you have researched at least an outline knowledge of your subject because that will then give you the hooks on which to hang further research.

As a productive person, remember that the main purpose of conducting research at the beginning stage of a project is to find the hooks for asking further questions.

3 ASK QUESTIONS

Asking questions is a major tool when you are talking to other people about a subject or when you are researching it. Important though it is to ask questions of other people, nevertheless the most important questions are the ones you ask yourself.

Use the questioning techniques in Chapters 5 and 6 to take the information you are receiving and process it in your mind so you open up new ideas to take the project forward. What you are aiming to do is to increase the number of hooks in your mind on which to hang further information and to increase the number of connections in your brain to illumine the path of action before you.

Every seed of information you sow in your brain will help to produce a harvest.

The one thing you do not want when you are taking a project forward is to restrict your ideas with plans or task lists. These are unfortunately very effective at freezing your thinking at a certain point and restricting development beyond it.

The tool to use instead of plans or task lists is the Dynamic List. At first glance this seems identical to the conventional task list for a particular project. But there is one big difference. A conventional task list is static and remains on file. It's edited as needed, but using the existing list as the starting point. A Dynamic List on the other hand is written out afresh each day when you start working on the project – without referring to any previous lists. You start the list with a few items and then add tasks as you think of them. In other words it is very similar to the Productivity Time Management System in the way it works.

The Dynamic List is actually a form of questioning. You are in effect asking yourself every day 'What are the actions I need to take now for this project?' This type of list encourages you to be creative at every stage without having to expend a great deal of mental energy in the process.

You can also use the Dynamic List as an emergency list. If you suddenly find yourself having to sort a situation out in a short time frame, you can launch yourself into action by simply writing down a few things that you need to do and then adding to it as you work. Don't underestimate the power of this.

Putting it all together

Talking about your project, doing research, asking questions of other people and yourself, using dynamic lists, plus the fact that the actual actions of your work will have effects sometimes a long time afterwards, are all ways of sowing the seeds that will produce results. Some of these seeds are directed at other people, some at your own thinking. They strengthen your connections in the world, and they strengthen the connections in your own mind.

Remember that the productive person, as we saw in Chapter 10, is in the process of growing their brain so that they can achieve what they set out to achieve. This means actual physical changes in the brain by growing connections. Each one of the 'seeds' I have mentioned above has this effect.

They also have the effect of making changes in the physical society around us. The world is full of connections waiting to be made. The productive person is the one who makes these connections, and makes them work for them.

32 REAP HARVEST

The day of fortune is like a harvest day. We must be busy when the corn is ripe.

Torquato Tasso

I inherited that calm from my father, who was a farmer. You sow, you wait for good or bad weather, you harvest, but working is something you always need to do.

Miguel Indurain

Striving for success without hard work is like trying to harvest where you haven't planted.

David Bly

Even after a bad harvest there must be sowing.

Seneca

There would be no advantage to be gained by sowing a field of wheat if the harvest did not return more than was sown.

Napoleon Hill

When you take on a challenging project you usually go through something like the following four stages. The process is not always quite as clear cut as this and different people will react differently, but on the whole it's a rough guide to the sort of development that you will go through.

First stage: You feel overwhelmed and are struggling. This is particularly likely to be the case if you have been put into a post with greater responsibilities than you are used to, or if you are dealing with situations which you have not experienced before.

Second stage: You start to find your feet. What seemed overwhelming and threatening at first is now becoming more familiar. Bit by bit you are making the mental connections which you need in order to function properly. You are beginning to make your own decisions without having to ask other people for help.

Third stage: You are doing an adequate job. You are able to function with competence, and you are regarded as reasonably competent by your co-workers. You have enough confidence in your own abilities to take action without being indecisive.

Fourth stage: You are hit by the realization that you know more about your subject than anyone else. It may only be a very limited field, but you are actually the world expert on how to do your job. No one knows more about it than you do.

It is in this fourth stage where you begin to reap the harvest of what you have sown previously. But you can't reach this stage without going through the previous stages. They are all essential to the process.

1 DON'T GET IMPATIENT

There are no shortcuts to this process. It's easy to get impatient and when this happens we are tempted either to get discouraged or else to take premature action.

The stages described above can be applied to a lot of life situations. For instance, you might decide to learn a foreign language which is unrelated to any you are already familiar with. In the first stage, the language seems to have no meaning at all, there are no hooks to hang new information on, you can't even pick out the sounds. It is however while you are in this stage that you will make the greatest advances in the shortest time. You start to get somewhat familiar with the sounds and rhythms even if you can't understand what is being said. You learn some of the common words and can hear them being used. You learn a little grammar and how some simple sentences are made. You are starting to construct the edifice. After only a few weeks, when you look back at Lesson 1 in your textbook what seemed incredibly daunting now seems easy.

Most people will get to this stage without much problem, provided they made any sort of serious resolution to learn the language in question. If they didn't get this far, it was probably because they were just dabbling without any serious intent.

But many people find it difficult to get beyond this stage. They start to get stuck. It isn't because the language gets more difficult after this. It's because they are not experiencing the sense of achievement they experienced in the first couple of weeks. In the first week or so they felt that they had learned a lot and now they expect to get a similar feeling every week. Unfortunately this is not what happens. Progress from now on seems to get slower and slower. In fact they are making just as much progress but it's a smaller proportion compared to the total of what they've already done.

In any endeavour if you make ten units of progress in the first week and another ten in the second week, you will have increased your progress 100 per cent in the second week. That's going to make you feel really good about your progress.

But after a month, when you've make 40 units of progress, the next week's work is only going to increase your progress by another 25 per cent. And after a year when you've made 520 units of progress, one week's further work is only going to add another 2 per cent. You are in reality still making progress at the same rate, but it appears to you as if you are getting constantly diminishing returns.

This is the danger point.

2 KEEP PLODDING ON

It would probably be an exaggeration to say that the difference between a productive person and a not so productive person is the ability to keep going after this danger point has been reached.

No, on second thoughts it wouldn't be an exaggeration. To be a productive person you need to be able to keep plodding on even when you are not receiving much reinforcement in terms of perceived progress. This quality is called persistence and is one of the most essential qualities that you can have in terms of real achievement.

The bad news is that persistence is not a quality that most people are born with.

The good news is that persistence comes with practice and can be achieved by anyone who sets their mind to it. It may be difficult at first but like any skill it improves the more you do it.

Remember the productive person's mantra: *Consistent regular focused attention is the key to success.* Practise giving things consistent regular focused attention and see what happens. Whatever you give this attention to will change, and so will you.

3 USE YOUR NEW MASTERY

As you use consistent regular focused attention so you will gradually achieve mastery in your endeavours. This will happen in a matter of days for some subjects and in a matter of years, sometime many years, for others.

To be a productive person the fundamental mastery you need to achieve is the ability to operate your time management system without needing to think about it. This doesn't mean that you don't need to think about what you are going to do, but that thinking what you are going to do is based on a system which is as near as possible invisible.

The Productivity Time Management method I propose in Chapter 9 uses all the principles of productivity and is the one I recommend. I've found it to be better and more reliable than any other system I have come across (including other ones I have developed myself). If you combine this system with randomizing (Chapter 38) and/or time boxing (Chapter 34), then you have some really powerful methods of getting things done at your disposal.

With this system as the basis for your action, you can go on to develop routines and systems in other areas. Remember that productive action needs a foundation of well-established and well-practised routines and systems.

There is really never an end to practice because even when you have reached the highest standard it is still important to build in a degree of redundancy. 'Redundancy' is an important concept in training. It means that you train to a higher standard than you are called on to use in most situations. That achieves two things. The first is that in normal situations you are only exercising a fraction of your skills and ability. The second is that when an emergency or exceptional situation occurs you can still respond to it within your capacity. An example of redundancy training is the training of airline pilots on simulators so that they are able to deal with a whole variety of emergency situations which they wouldn't otherwise meet in a lifetime's experience of flying.

Putting it all together

Looking at the quotations at the beginning of this chapter, you can see three things stand out clearly.

1. To be able to reap the harvest, you must put in the necessary work beforehand.
2. The return is much greater than what it would have been if you'd skimped or omitted the preparatory work.
3. If you want to continue reaping you need to continue sowing.

All these three need your attention. To neglect any one of them is to jeopardize the work you put into the other two.

AIDS TO PRODUCTIVITY

In this section we look at some additional aids which though not strictly part of the productivity process can be used as much or as little as you like to supplement it.

MAKE THE MOST OF TECHNOLOGY

The first rule of any technology used in a business is that automation applied to an efficient operation will magnify the efficiency. The second is that automation applied to an inefficient operation will magnify the inefficiency.
Bill Gates

The number one benefit of information technology is that it empowers people to do what they want to do. It lets people be creative. It lets people be productive. It lets people learn things they didn't think they could learn before, and so in a sense it is all about potential.
Steve Ballmer

The typewriting machine, when played with expression, is no more annoying than the piano when played by a sister or near relation.
Oscar Wilde

Before you become too entranced with gorgeous gadgets and mesmerizing video displays, let me remind you that information is not knowledge, knowledge is not wisdom, and wisdom is not foresight. Each grows out of the other, and we need them all.
Arthur C. Clarke

Truth is emotional, it's fluid, and above all, it's human. No matter how quick we get with computers, no matter how much information we have, you'll never be able to remove the human from the truth-seeking exercise.
Markham Nolan

It's hardly necessary for me to tell you that we live in a world of technology. Or that you can use the internet, social media and the cloud to help your productivity. Such things are a given nowadays, though anyone who works with the general public will know that there are still plenty of people, in Western society mainly the elderly, who don't have a computer and are not on email, let alone anything more sophisticated.

Those of us who started work when there were no voicemail, photocopiers, or personal computers, let alone smartphones and social media, can remember how each of these inventions brought a revolution to our working practices.

Nevertheless none of these have affected the principles of productivity. We may have better instruments to work with, but the principles remain the same. To paraphrase Bill Gates in the quotation at the head of this chapter, technology magnifies the effectiveness of effective processes, but also magnifies the ineffectiveness of ineffective processes.

Technology should be a servant not a master. It can easily become a master if we allow it to. It gives us great freedom in many ways, but also has an addictive quality about it which can take over our lives. How do we keep it in its place? By remembering why we are using it. In Chapter 19 I described the method of keeping two goals lined up – a nearer and a further one – to prevent the nearer one from developing a life of its own. It is exactly the same with technology. For instance we are less likely to get overwhelmed by email if we keep in sight why we are using email in the first place – for speed and efficiency of communication.

In this chapter I will be talking about technology as applied to personal productiveness, not technology in industrial processes which is outside the scope of this book. However we've all come across plenty of cases in which technology used by big business is actually defeating the purpose for which it was installed – just think of the words 'call centre'. When we have to develop technology to keep the technology at bay there is something seriously wrong.

We need to be careful not to fall into the same trap where our personal productivity is concerned. However much we use technology, we should keep the immediate goal lined up with one of our higher-level commitments.

1 USE TECHNOLOGY TO SPEED UP PROCESSES

As I have said many times throughout this book, good processes are the basis of productivity. Whatever the field, technology can be a major factor in the development of these processes.

To give one very simple illustration, as I type the first draft of this book my word processor is giving me instant feedback at the bottom of the screen on my word count for the book so far (49,651 words in total, 93 so far today). This is something so trivial these days that we hardly think about it, yet keeping track of the word count for a book forty years ago would have been a cumbersome and onerous process. Today I can use it easily to check that I am on course for finishing the book on time.

Sometime later today I will go for a walk, and I will track the distance and speed with my phone. I can then compare the statistics with previous days. There are many other apps which can help with fitness and health, including pulse monitoring, and exercise routines. There are even apps which will fine you real money if you do not keep to your schedule!

Apps abound for to-do lists, timers, learning vocabulary and facts, calorie counting, processing email, and so on and so forth. In fact you only have to think of an activity and there will be an app for it, and it will probably synchronize between all your devices without any problem.

My main concern is with apps that help with processes and routines and the most important of these for this purpose are the ones that help you to keep track of your progress. This makes it easy to ensure that your routines are producing improvement in your life and work.

2 USE TECHNOLOGY FOR CREATIVITY AND RESEARCH

It's a commonplace that the internet is a great place for doing research, though the quality of some of the material on offer is dubious. One source which is often neglected is that it may be possible to discuss books and articles with their authors on their websites. They will often spend a considerable amount of time answering genuine enquiries, and other posters on site forums can be very knowledgeable too.

A note-taking application like Evernote can make it very easy to collect articles and other sources of information. You can easily gather a vast amount of information and make it easy to find related content. Evernote is also useful for reminders, sharing information, and keeping to-do lists. It will read and index writing in graphics so it is ideal for taking pictures of signs, notices, menus, and the like and then being able to search the text in them. Evernote is also an excellent place to write and store your answers to the questioning techniques I describe in Chapters 5 and 6.

Whether or not you use a note-taking app like Evernote, there are all sorts of ways in which the camera on a smartphone can be used, such as taking pictures of people at a conference with their name tags so you have a visual record of the people you've met – and to which you can add notes. Or if you're worried about forgetting where you've left your car in a multi-storey, just take a photo of the signs showing the floor and row. You can scan documents on the fly pretty successfully with a smartphone too.

As for reading books, a Kindle now allows you to skim through a book, refer directly to Wikipedia from the text, and have a directly accessible dictionary in which you can look up a word in English or a foreign language.

If you read this book in three or four years' time, what I have written here in 2015 will almost certainly seem laughably out of date. But whatever technology has been developed in the future, the productive person will still be using questions like 'What are be the top five ways I could use this?', 'What needs do I have that might have an application that can help?', or even 'What needs do people have that I could design an application for?'

Remember that technology must be the servant not the master. Just because something *can* be done through technology doesn't necessarily mean that it *has* to be done that way – or that it's best done that way. For instance, many people including myself still prefer pen and paper for such things as lists, notes at lectures, and so on. Handwriting has a much more direct effect on the memory than writing with a keyboard. Of course I can still take a photo of my handwritten notes with my phone and Evernote will then read my handwriting.

3 USE TECHNOLOGY FOR COMMUNICATIONS

As well as speeding up processes and making creativity and research vastly easier, a third way in which technology has brought huge change into our lives is communication. We can communicate with our friends and family at all times and in all places, but we can also communicate with the world at large or at least a fair-sized chunk of it. My own coaching business was almost entirely built up using the internet, which meant that I had clients from all around the world. As long as their English was sufficiently good it was as easy for me to coach someone in Sweden, Russia or California as it was to coach people living in England. I often used to reflect on the fact that my work would have been literally impossible if I had had to use the technology which was available to me when I was an employee.

Like other forms of technology communication is a two-edged weapon. One of the most common reasons people seek advice from time management experts is to help them deal with the pressure of constant emails, text messages, voicemail and so on. Paper, which made up the bulk of most office workers' work not so long along ago, is seen as a secondary problem. Most paper arrives electronically now and is printed out, so it too has become part of the communications revolution.

The solution as I mentioned in the introduction to this chapter is to remember why we are using communications in the first place, so that we can prevent it taking on a life of its own. It is very easy for this to happen once we start using communications aimlessly. This can best be avoided by constant review and questioning.

Putting it all together

There is no reason to suppose that technology is going to stop developing into a sharper and sharper two-edged sword. As its usefulness increases so its temptations will increase too. Psychologists are concerned that it is making major changes in the way we think. In a few years from now the world of work will be hit by a generation which has been using smartphones and tablets since they were babies. Things may be very different then.

Perhaps the most important factor for the future is one which I very rarely hear mentioned. We have become entirely dependent on power supplies in a way which previous generations have not been. We need electricity to work our computers, charge our phones, control our thermostats, work shop tills, and organize deliveries. With increasing uncertainty in the sourcing of energy, this could mean that only people who are resourceful enough to adapt to rapidly changing circumstances are likely to prosper. This is another good reason why you need to have the productive mindset, so that you can make use of technology to the full but be able to survive without it.

34 SUPERCHARGE YOUR TIME MANAGEMENT WITH TIME BOXING

Don't count every hour in the day, make every hour in the day count.
Isak Dinesen

Yesterday is a cancelled check; tomorrow is a promissory note; today is the only cash you have - so spend it wisely.
Kay Lyons

Defer no time, delays have dangerous ends.
William Shakespeare

Don't say you don't have enough time. You have exactly the same number of hours per day that were given to Helen Keller, Pasteur, Michaelangelo, Mother Teresa, Leonardo da Vinci, Thomas Jefferson, and Albert Einstein.
H. Jackson Brown, Jr.

You may delay, but time will not.
Benjamin Franklin

The term 'time boxing' may or may not be familiar to you. It describes a technique for concentrating your work by using timed bursts. These bursts can vary in length, though they are usually short enough to be described in minutes rather than hours.

Although the name 'time boxing' is relatively new, the method itself is as old as the hills. A forty-minute school lesson is a good example of a 'time box'. In the school lesson one subject is studied intensively for exactly forty minutes. At the end of the period the class stops work on the subject and takes a break before either resuming or doing something else.

In this type of environment class members tend to remember best what comes at the beginning of the class and what comes at the end. That's why good teachers will start a lesson by briefly revising the previous lesson, and end it by summarizing what has just been covered.

The school lesson is an example of a time box that you will almost certainly have experienced. You can use exactly the same principle in your work by concentrating on a specific subject for a pre-determined length of time. As we shall see, the pre-determined time doesn't have to be forty minutes. It can be almost any length because the result will be the same whether it's five minutes or forty minutes – or even longer.

The overall effect is not only to concentrate your work, but also to give you an extra burst of energy at the start and at the end of the period. It doesn't matter how long or short the period is, just so long as the finish time is clearly known. The effect of stopping dead at the finish time works with a burst of a few minutes, but also for periods of weeks or even months. For instance the concentrating effect is noticeable as you start to clear your desk before the weekend. And it's particularly noticeable just before you leave for a holiday. Although these are illustrations of the same effect, we wouldn't normally use the term 'time boxing' to describe them.

My first book *Get Everything Done and Still Have Time to Play* dealt in detail with various methods of using time boxing (though the term itself wasn't used then).

In your own work, time boxing can be used in a variety of ways. Short time boxes are especially effective in overcoming procrastination. Longer time boxes are effective in helping you to concentrate your work.

1 TIME BOX THE TASKS

Time boxing your tasks can add another dimension of concentration to your work. There are a wide variety of methods, which vary in intensity. My own practice these days is to use time boxing only when I feel I need it, usually when I'm feeling more distracted than usual. Because it tends to be quite intense it's best not to keep it up for long periods. It's quite possible to use it for one important project, say a writing project, without using it for other tasks. An opposite way to use it is for getting small tasks out of the way as quickly as possible.

When using time boxing there are three variables to consider:

1. The length of burst
2. The number tasks that are being worked on
3. The gap between bursts

I'll give a few examples of how these variables can be used. They are only examples and you can be as creative as you like with the variables.

Example 1: Use an increasing length of burst starting with one minute and then increasing by one minute each time. So the bursts would be one minute, two minutes, three minutes, four minutes and so on up to 15 minutes. After that you can count back down to one minute again if you wish. You work on one task only and there is no gap between bursts. This is amazingly (and quite surprisingly) effective. You really can't appreciate the effect unless you try it. A variation is to start with a 15-minute burst and then work down to a one-minute burst.

Example 2: Use bursts with a number of tasks. I often use this with increasing bursts of five minutes, ten minutes, 15 minutes and so on. With three tasks it would go like this: five minutes on Task A, five minutes on Task B, five minutes on Task C, ten minutes on Task A, ten minutes on Task B and so on. When a new task replaces one that has been completed, it starts from five minutes, while the remaining unfinished tasks carry on increasing their burst length. A variation is not to use increasing bursts but a fixed burst length throughout, say 20 minutes.

Example 3: Use a longer length of time box, say 20 minutes, for one task only. Take a rest of five minutes between bursts. During the rest period you can do anything you like except work on the task. This is particularly effective with lengthy tasks that require some deep concentration, such as studying or writing a book, report or article. Give yourself a target to attain, such as reading so many pages or writing so many words. Once you've attained the target, move on to something else.

While I'm talking about targets I'll mention that it's more motivating to count down to a target ('I've got 450 words to go') rather than count up to it ('I've written 550 words').

One problem with time boxing is that it requires some sort of alarm, so it may be difficult to use it in a shared office situation especially when you are using short time periods. You may be able to get round this by using a visual or vibrating alarm rather than an audible one. There are plenty of alarm applications available, so shop around a bit.

Not all tasks are suitable for time boxing of course. There are many tasks which need to be done in one go and can't be chopped up into smaller pieces. However, these tasks may need preparation and tidying up afterwards and these parts can be time boxed. The rule is to time box the task until you hit the part that needs to be done in one go, and then recommence time boxing when you get to the tidying-up.

2 TIME BOX THE GAPS

One of my favourite uses for time boxing is not for working on tasks, but on the gaps between them.

In my experience, the time I am most likely to get distracted is after I've finished a task and before I start the next one. Once my mind has registered the fact that I've finished a task, there's a tendency for me to want to take a short break. A short break of course can only too easily become a long break. This delay in getting back to work can also be a danger after an interruption, such as a phone call or an unscheduled visit by a colleague to discuss a project. In both cases there's a danger of faffing around for a long period doing nothing in particular.

An effective way of stopping gaps or interruptions going on for too long is to time box them. As soon as I finish a task, I start my timer. I then use a one-minute, two-minute, three-minute sequence. Each time the alarm goes off I am reminded that I haven't yet got back to the task I'm supposed to be doing. I keep resetting the timer until I'm working when it goes off. Once that happens I know there's no need to reset it again – until the next time of course.

3 TIME BOX LEISURE

As well as concentrating work, time boxing also concentrates leisure. If you decide to take a break, then set an exact time for it to finish. In the same way that it's important to stop working at the end of a time box, so it's important to start working again at the end of a break. The effectiveness of both the work and the break is greatly reduced if you do not stop or start exactly when the time is due. Don't allow yourself to be tempted to 'finish something off'. Stop mid-sentence if need be.

When you are working you should be doing nothing except work. During a break you can do anything except work. You will find that both your work and your break benefit from this clear demarcation. A break that is treated as a time box is far more relaxing than taking a break when you feel like it and drifting back to work when you feel like it.

Putting it all together

As an exercise, try one or more of the following:

1. Take a routine task that you don't particularly like doing and try the one-minute, two-minute, three-minute, etc, technique on it. Make sure that you have a method of signalling the end of the interval which won't disturb other people in your vicinity. Remember that in this method you take no breaks between the intervals. You just work straight on.

2. Take two tasks which will take a bit of time to do and try alternating them using the five-minute, ten-minute, 15-minute, etc, technique. If this works for you, try it again with three tasks.

3. Take a longer task which will take some concentrated thought, such as writing an article or blog post. Work on it for intervals of 20 minutes, with a five-minute rest in between each one. Don't forget to time the rests as well as the work periods.

4. Take a mid-morning break of exactly 20 minutes. Start work again immediately the alarm goes off. During the break you can do anything you like as long as it isn't work. Be strict about this.

There'll be a lot more about breaks and related matters in the next chapter.

35 TAKE BREAKS AND NAPS

*There is more refreshment and stimulation in a nap,
even of the briefest, than in all the alcohol ever distilled.*
Ovid

When the going gets tough, the tough take a nap.
Tom Hodgkinson

No day is so bad it can't be fixed with a nap.
Carrie Snow

*Keep close to Nature's heart... and break clear away,
once in awhile, and climb a mountain or spend a week
in the woods. Wash your spirit clean.*
John Muir

*We spend our lives searching for meaning. Take a break.
Let it find you.*
Dan McCoy

Working productively is by its very nature less stressful and demanding than the way most people work. This is because the first step in being productive is to gain control of one's life by establishing systems and routines that simplify the ordinary business of daily living. The result is that there is minimum background friction, which frees one up to concentrate on really productive work. Productivity also involves reducing commitments to a level that you have time to handle properly. The result is that you can remain on top of your work – which in itself is a great source of energy.

To work effectively another factor is that it is essential to get enough rest and to take adequate breaks during your work. As I've said several times already, adequate breaks mean you get more work done, not less.

Oddly enough, one of the problems with being truly productive is that it can look as if you are doing less work than unproductive people. For example, one of the most essential activities for productive people is thinking. Unfortunately sitting in your office calmly thinking looks far less like work than rushing around with a clip-board, complaining about how much work you have. As for taking a nap, that is positively inviting people to consider you as lazy even though you may in fact be doing many times more productive work than they are.

I learned very early on in my work life that the really effective people were the ones who spent as much time and energy on their leisure pursuits as they did on their work. Their motto was 'Work hard, play hard'. The people who never took any time off, and could regularly be found working late into the evening and at weekends were seldom the ones thought of most highly by their colleagues and superiors.

1 TAKE POWER NAPS

There are basically two types of nap. The scheduled ones and the unscheduled ones.

The classic example of the scheduled nap is the siesta. Winston Churchill according to his own account discovered the great benefit of the siesta when acting as a war correspondent with the Spanish Army in Cuba in 1895.

By this time hammocks had been slung between the trees of a thicket. Into these hammocks we were now enjoined to retire. The soldiers and regimental officers extended themselves upon the ground after, I trust, taking the necessary military precautions, and every one slept in the shade for about four hours.

At two o'clock the siesta was over. Bustle arose in the silent midday bivouac. At three in the afternoon we were once more on the way, and marched four hours at a speed of certainly not less than 2 miles an hour. As dusk was falling we reached our camping ground for the night. The column had covered 18 or 19 miles, and the infantry did not seem in the least fatigued. These tough Spanish peasants, sons of the soil, could jog along with heavy loads over mere tracks with an admirable persistence. The prolonged midday halt was like a second night's rest to them.

... The rest and the spell of sleep in the middle of the day refresh the human frame far more than a long night. We were not made by Nature to work, or even to play, from eight o'clock in the morning till midnight. We throw a strain upon our system which is unfair and improvident. For every purpose of business or pleasure, mental or physical, we ought to break our days and our marches into two. When I was at the Admiralty in the War, I found I could add nearly two hours to my working effort by going to bed for an hour after luncheon.

(from *My Early Life*, Chapter VI Cuba)

The unscheduled nap may not be quite as effective but is easier to put into practice – at least in those countries which don't still keep the tradition of the siesta. All it consists of is taking a nap whenever your concentration starts to slip or you begin to feel sleepy. The length of the nap can be as short as ten minutes. Most people find about 20 minutes to be the best. Too long a nap can leave you feeling groggy. You can experiment to find the best length of time for you – which of course has to take into account the circumstances in which you are working.

A short nap is also very effective if you are feeling sleepy while driving. Instead of trying to push on, pull off the road and go to sleep for ten minutes. You will probably find that the feeling of sleepiness has disappeared when the nap is over. Only a short break is needed to make your driving a lot safer.

2 TIMED BREAKS

Breaks are like naps except that they don't involve going to sleep. Instead they involve stopping work and freewheeling for a period of time. You can do whatever you like as long as it isn't work. Like naps, breaks can be scheduled or unscheduled. If you are in a situation where it's impossible to take a nap, then take a break instead. But make sure you set a time to start work again – it will be much more refreshing if you do.

Scheduled breaks

There are two essential rules which I always recommend for people who work in an office away from home. People who work at home can be little more flexible, but the same principles apply.

1. The first rule is: *Always finish work at the same time every day*. It doesn't matter what the time is so much as the fact that it is a definite time. I call the way that a definite stop concentrates your work 'the end effect'.
2. The second rule is: *Take a fixed lunch break*. Working through lunch achieves little except to lower the quality of your work for the rest of the day. By having a defined time for starting your lunch break and a defined time for finishing it you achieve two end effects, one for work and one for leisure. During lunch break you can do whatever you like as long as it isn't work.

Those are the two most important rules, but there are several more you can build into your work day.

3. Take a 20–30 minute break mid-morning and another mid-afternoon. This is a good way to keep yourself refreshed during the day.
4. Take a 5–10 minute break after you've worked for 40 minutes. This gives you several additional end effects.

If you apply all four of these rules, you might end up with a timetable which looks something like this:

0900–0940 Work Period 1

0950–1030 Work Period 2

1100–1140 Work Period 3

1150–1230 Work Period 4

1400–1440 Work Period 5

1450–1530 Work Period 6

1600–1640 Work Period 7

1650–1730 Work Period 8

If this sounds familiar, it's the exact timetable which my old school and many others used to use. When I joined the Army I found virtually the same timetable being used there. Have you ever noticed how long the days seemed during school and how much work got done during them compared to what you do now?

It's also the timetable many seminars and conferences follow. Again the day seems long and a lot seems to get done, especially by comparison with the frenetic unstructured pace of a typical office day. One of the most common things people say at the office is 'I can't believe it. It's already 4 o'clock and I haven't done a thing'. I've never heard anyone say that at a conference.

3 DEPTH ACTIVITIES

It's important to have activities in your life which don't relate to work. Chosen properly, these will give depth and meaning to your life. This in turn will positively affect your work.

The most important of these depth activities from the point of general health and well-being is exercise. It's easy to forget that your brain is part of your body and anything which affects your body negatively will affect your brain negatively too. Conversely anything which affects your body positively will affect your brain positively. When I was at school there was a Latin motto prominently displaying in the gym, '*Mens sana in corpore sano*' ('A healthy mind in a healthy body'). The motto is no longer there, but the advice is still good.

Exercise does not need to be elaborate for the purposes of health and well-being. A 20-minute brisk walk at least three or four times a week goes a long way. As with anything else it's important to remember *why* you are exercising in the first place.

Generally speaking, the motto 'Work hard, play hard' applies to depth activities. Whatever you do, take it as seriously as you take your work. Develop systems and routines so that it becomes easy to do. Question the situation and learn about it. For instance, a holiday becomes much more enjoyable if you have done some basic research on the history and economics of the country. Engage with life actively, rather than being a passive spectator.

Putting it all together

If you've got one message from this chapter, it should be that productivity is not only about work. Rest and recreation are essential parts of keeping yourself at maximum effectiveness. The brain is part of the body and everything that affects the body will also affect the brain.

Not only that but rest and recreation are much more effective and enjoyable when approached in a productive way. Having a productive attitude is a desirable thing in itself and can link all the strands of your life together in a meaningful way to lead a happy and fulfilled life.

36 BEAT YOUR PERSONAL AVERAGE, NOT YOUR PERSONAL BEST

The reason we struggle with insecurity is because we compare our behind-the-scenes with everyone else's highlight reel.

Steve Furtick

We cannot become what we want to be by remaining what we are.

Max DePree

It's no use saying, 'We are doing our best.' You have got to succeed in doing what is necessary.

Winston Churchill

Unless you're continually improving your skills, you're quickly becoming irrelevant.

Stephen Covey

We should not judge people by their peak of excellence; but by the distance they have travelled from the point where they started.

Henry Ward Beecher

I've written a lot in this book about raising standards by meticulously monitoring our progress. This obviously implies that over time one should be getting better and better.

What is the best way to monitor this progress?

Usually when people talk about monitoring their progress they are thinking in terms of aiming to beat their current personal best. Hitting a new personal best is a matter for celebration and gives feeling of achievement. A new personal best is good when it arrives, but it's not actually what we should be monitoring.

Constantly trying to beat your personal best can easily lead to over-exertion and can have the effect of building up so much resistance that you can hardly drag yourself to do your practice. You will in short be setting yourself up to fail because sooner or later you will find the strain so great that you simply give up. What's more, if it's exercise that you are monitoring all you may achieve is to injure yourself.

There is a much easier way than aiming to beat your personal best. It leads to just as good results and allows you to practise at a level which is well within your capabilities and keeps your motivation going.

This better way is to aim to beat your personal average each time you practise.

1 AIM TO BEAT YOUR PERSONAL AVERAGE

Aiming to beat your personal average produces every bit as good results as aiming to beat your personal best. What's more it doesn't involve forcing yourself to go further or faster than you feel really capable of doing. Nevertheless if you concentrate on beating your personal average, you *will* also keep beating your personal best – but without the pressure.

As an example from my own personal experience, I used this method after a serious illness to increase my fitness by walking. I walked three or four times a week. In nineteen walks I increased my average distance every time. My first walk was only one mile – my nineteenth was seven miles.

Now here's something interesting. During the 19 walks I beat my personal best nine times. This is probably at least as good a result as I would have got had the personal best been what I had actually been aiming to beat. The difference was that I never felt any pressure to go beyond what I felt I could easily do.

I knew that my personal average was well within my capabilities and I never had any doubt about my ability to raise it every day. On most days I went well beyond it. But it would have been too taxing to try to beat my personal best each day. I would have got discouraged whenever I didn't succeed in beating it, especially if that went on for several days.

Aiming to beat my personal average resulted in chalking up a success for every one of those 19 walks. But during those walks I twice went for four walks in a row without beating my personal best. If I'd had my personal best as the target, each of those days would have been marked up in my mind as a failure.

What at root makes the personal average a better target than the personal best is that it quickly builds up a series of small successes. It's quite possible for anyone to beat their personal average every day as I did. Success builds on success, so you are opening the way to further improvement. On the other hand it simply isn't possible for anyone to beat their personal best every day. That means inevitably that aiming to beat your personal best is going to chalk up a large number of failures. Just as success breeds success, so failure breeds failure.

2 EXTEND THE NUMBER OF THINGS YOU USE THIS FOR

You can use the personal average method to increase or decrease (or even keep the same) virtually anything that you can put a number on. It doesn't have to be some mighty Olympian feat of endurance – it can be used for quite ordinary things.

For instance weight loss methods often depend on losing a pound or so a week. If you haven't lost the requisite amount at the end of the week, you feel as if you are a failure. And yet this may not be the case at all because one's weight can vary naturally to quite a considerable extent. A more effective method would be to weigh yourself daily and aim to keep lowering your average weight.

At one time I used the personal average method to get out of the bad habit of going to bed late. I kept track of the time I went to bed by counting minutes after midnight as a positive number and minutes before midnight as a negative number. This worked very effectively.

If you want to spend a certain number of hours a day on an activity like studying, practising a musical instrument or learning a foreign language, then it's a good idea to work up to it slowly using the personal average method to measure the time.

You might also try it on your finances. I've already mentioned in Chapter 30 how I monitor my cash flow on a daily basis. It would be a simple matter to use the personal average to improve the balance. In a similar way you could use it to monitor your levels of debt, your earnings or any one of hundreds of other indicators.

Particularly with exercise, it can get boring if you go after the same indicator day after day. One way to vary it is to alternate between number and speed.

For example after I'd got my walking distance up to seven miles, I could then have stopped increasing the distance and instead concentrated for a period on increasing the speed at which I could do five miles. Once I'd improved that, I could then go back to increasing distance.

Another example from the world of exercise would be to work at increasing the total number of push ups you can do for a week and then work at increasing the speed at which you can do a set number for another week.

3 MAINTAIN YOUR PERSONAL AVERAGE WHEN YOU HAVE REACHED YOUR TARGET

When you reach the level you are happy with (or you just want to go onto maintenance while you concentrate on something else) stop aiming to increase or decrease your personal average, and instead aim to hold it steady. Keep a record of your average as before and adjust your activity whenever it goes lower or higher.

You need to reset the average regularly because the longer the time period you are basing it on, the less sensitive it is to recent movements. It's possible to use a moving average, but I'm not particularly fond of those because whether you are higher or lower than the average is just a question of whether your current measurement is higher or lower than the first number in the series. That gives too much of a temptation to game the system.

Putting it all together

The personal average is a very versatile method of improving your performance. You can use it in virtually any field so long as you can find at least one numerical indicator to track. It's highly motivating because you can claim a success nearly every day and still be confident that you are advancing at a good pace.

Whether it's physical exercise, studying, practising, ameliorating your finances, as long as you can find a number to track you can use the personal average to make your life better.

37 CONCENTRATE ON THE PROCESS

Excellence is a continuous process and not an accident.
A.P.J. Abdul Kalam

The most difficult thing is the decision to act, the rest is merely tenacity. The fears are paper tigers. You can do anything you decide to do. You can act to change and control your life; and the procedure, the process is its own reward.
Amelia Earhart

If you can't describe what you are doing as a process, you don't know what you're doing.
W. Edwards Deming

The advice I like to give young artists, or really anybody who'll listen to me, is not to wait around for inspiration. Inspiration is for amateurs; the rest of us just show up and get to work. If you wait around for the clouds to part and a bolt of lightning to strike you in the brain, you are not going to make an awful lot of work. All the best ideas come out of the process; they come out of the work itself. Things occur to you. If you're sitting around trying to dream up a great art idea, you can sit there a long time before anything happens. But if you just get to work, something will occur to you and something else will occur to you and something else that you reject will push you in another direction. Inspiration is absolutely unnecessary and somehow deceptive. You feel like you need this great idea before you can get down to work, and I find that's almost never the case.
Chuck Close

Art was as much in the activity as in the results. Works of art were not just the finished product, but the thought, the action, the process that created them.
Jean M. Auel

What I've been saying throughout this book is that productivity is not a matter of inspiration or a characteristic that you are born with, but a process. If you want to be productive in the same way that Isaac Newton, Vincent van Gogh and Henry Ford were productive, then it is a matter of finding the right process and sticking to it.

Of course you won't find the right process, let alone stick to it, until you make up your mind that you want to be productive. It is up to you in what parts of your life you apply the principles of productivity. You can use them to make your life better in the way you want, not in the way that other people want you to.

In this book, I've described a process that works. I've no doubt whatsoever that it can be improved, but you cannot ignore the fact that you need a process. If you stick to the process, then you *will* be more productive – just as you *will* be stronger if you do push-ups every day. If you just read about it out of interest and dabble with it for a few days, then you will be no more productive than you would be stronger if you did a couple of days' worth of push ups and then forgot all about exercising.

Basically there are three parts to the process of productivity:

1 USE QUESTIONS FOR CREATIVITY

To be genuinely creative it is essential to question the environment in which you find yourself. You can use some or all of the question methods given in Chapters 5 and 6. Creativity is one of the two major factors in productivity. Without creativity productivity is often reduced to being a matter of churning out work without any real thought about where it is going or what it is for.

The essential parts of questioning are:

1. **Ask the right questions:** The first question you should ask is what the most important questions you should be asking yourself are. Identifying these questions is an extremely good exercise with which to start your newly productive life. And you should come back to it at intervals along the way.

2. **Questioning only works when you begin to answer the questions:** Posing questions is not enough. It's only when you start trying to answer them that your mind kicks into gear and starts really working on them. Unfortunately it's surprisingly common for someone to ask a question, but never to get as far as attempting to answer it. How many times for instance have you asked yourself a question like 'Why am I always late for meetings?' without actually investigating what the reasons really are?

3. **Answering questions needs maturation:** The way to generate creative answers to a question is to make a first shot at answering it and then come back to it daily for a period of a week or more. Chapter 6 contains several techniques for doing this. Once you have chosen the best answers and started working on them, new horizons will open up which will generate further questions.

2 MANAGE YOUR TIME EFFICIENTLY

The time management system in Chapter 9 has been carefully designed to enable three things:

1 Make use of questioning

You have to ask yourself many times during the day what it's most important for you to do next. Each day you repeat this process. This is a case of using questioning to build up a firm daily foundation for your actions.

2 Develop routines which will become second nature

You will find that the result of the daily questioning is that you build up a daily routine which works smoothly to deal with the normal daily low-level matters like email, and also adapts well to major projects as they arrive.

3 Counteract the natural tendency to expand one's commitments

The most important characteristic of the Productivity Time Management system is that it only includes tasks which you have actually done. That means it provides a reality check on what you can succeed in doing during one day's work.

3 DON'T LET YOUR FOCUS SLIP

What achieves results is the amount of focused attention that you give a project. Once that focus is allowed to slip, your results will slip too. The most common cause of loss of focus is over-commitment. It is simply not possible to maintain focus if you have more commitments than you have time for.

If you adhere to the Productivity Time Management System you will succeed in keeping your list of commitments well weeded. You will find that most of the time this happens virtually automatically if you keep to the system. However you do need to check that what you are doing each day is what you actually need to be doing.

Alarm bells should go off in your head if you find that you are engaging in any activity without giving it sufficient regular focused attention.

Notice the two parts of this statement:

1. You are engaging in an activity
2. You are not giving it sufficient attention

This is a sure sign that you have lost focus with respect to at least one of your activities. Once you have lost focus over one activity there is a strong danger that this lost focus will spread to your other activities. There is a simple rule that you can follow in these circumstances:

If you are not giving a project sufficient regular focused attention you should stop doing it.

There's a very good reason for such drastic action. Time spent on a project which you are not doing properly is time which could have been spend on productive work. This is the trap which unproductive people fall into. They have a lot of projects which they are fooling around with, but the only result is that they don't have time to do any of their work properly.

Another way of bringing your focus back is to redefine the project in such a way that you do have time to do it. If your project is to clean your entire house every week, then you could redefine it so that your aim is to clean it every two weeks. Or you could clean the main living rooms once a week and the less used rooms once a month. Or you could employ someone to do the cleaning, leaving only tidying up as your own work. The choice is yours – but you do have to make the choice.

Putting it all together

Basically a lack of productivity is always caused by a system failure (see Chapter 4). Therefore the remedy is to look at your systems and processes. If you have worked these out properly then the cause of your lack of productivity is almost certainly that you haven't been keeping to the process. This is a serious matter because the essence of following any process is to practise it until it works without having to think about it. If you don't adhere to the system you are practising how *not* to do it properly.

This means that instead of practising how to be productive, you are practising how to be unproductive.

This emphasizes the importance of practising correctly. Whatever you practise is going to be reinforced – whether it is the right way or the wrong way. If in the past you have not been as productive as you would like, then that is because you have been practising doing things the wrong way for many years, and therefore the wrong way has been continually reinforced. Don't get impatient if it takes time to establish the right way of doing things. Persevere!

38 RANDOMNESS

Expose yourself to as much randomness as possible.
Ben Casnocha

There's a lot of randomness in the
decisions that people make.
Daniel Kahneman

I listen to Radio 4 and put the iPod on shuffle. I like the
randomness of, say, the Stones, then something from Nina
Simone, Nick Drake or Bob Dylan.
Catherine McCormack

To dare every day to be irreverent and bold. To dare to
preserve the randomness of mind which in children produces
strange and wonderful new thoughts and forms. To continually
scramble the familiar and bring the old into new juxtaposition.
Gordon Webber

Why did children seem to be so often spontaneous, joy-filled
and concentrated while adults seemed controlled, anxiety-
filled and diffused? It was the Goddam sense of having a self.
Luke Rhinehart

Making decisions can be stressful. When we make a decision
we feel responsible for the consequences of that decision. The
way it presents itself to our minds is that there is only one right
decision. All other decisions are wrong decisions. Only if we
make the one right decision will it turn out right. If we make
any of the possible wrong decisions then it will turn out wrong.
So it's not surprising that decision making becomes a stressful
activity for us.

What's more we have to make hundreds of minor decisions
throughout the day. This can become a very real source of

stress in our lives. Often people we think of as inefficient and unproductive are like that more because they find it too stressful to make decisions than for any other cause.

This is one reason why routines and systems are essential to productive living. While you are setting up a system you are making decisions about what that system should be, but once it's set up you don't have to make those decisions again. You just follow the system. You keep your energy for the higher-level creative work.

An additional way of removing the stress of decision making is to get the idea that there is only one right decision out of your mind. A typical example of this 'one right decision' thinking is found in those people who think that someone out there is the right life-partner, the person who is made for them. They are always chasing after an impossible dream because the 'right partner' simply does not exist. There are potential partners who are better than others certainly, but the trouble is that if you are convinced there is a *perfect* partner you are not going to be looking for a *good* partner. The result is either that you never settle down with anyone or you live in a permanent state of discontent with the person you do pick. Instead of working with a good partner to make a good life together, you reject what you have because you haven't got the perfect partner. The perfect partner of course comes with a ready-made perfect life which requires no work from you at all.

A good way of getting out of this poisonous way of thinking is to start making some minor decisions at random. You then live with the results of the decision. Doing this helps you to realize that there are no right or wrong decisions – just decisions with different results. Whatever the result of your decision you can deal with it.

Please be clear that I'm talking here about making small decisions about relatively routine matters as an exercise. I'm not suggesting making life-changing or illegal decisions at random. Please apply common sense and use responsibly!

1 REMOVE DECISION FATIGUE BY RANDOM CHOICE

The classic way of making random decisions is by the flip of a coin or the roll of a die, and these work just as well as ever they did. These days there is also an abundance of apps which can produce random numbers in a much more flexible way. The one I use is *Randomizers*, which uses white noise to produce random numbers which are genuinely random. It can select a random number from any sized set of numbers, rather than just two using a coin or six using a die.

By the way, I want to give you a word of caution about using *two* dice. Not everyone realizes this, but if you use two dice the odds are not the same for all the results. For example it's nearly six times more likely that you'll throw a 7 than a 12. But of course you knew that already, didn't you?

An exercise

For the next three days make a list of minor tasks you would like to get done. Each day make the list slightly longer than you are likely to be able to finish within the day. Then take action on the tasks as follows:

> **Day 1:** In whatever order you like.
>
> **Day 2:** In the order they are written.
>
> **Day 3:** In random order selected by your random number generator

Compare how you felt each day. Which felt easier? Which day did you get the most work done? Which day did you get the most important tasks done?

For a randomizer to have the right effect on your mind you must not fail to take action on the choice which it has made. So it is important that you are actually prepared to do whatever choices you put on the list. If you ignore the decision of the randomizer then your mind will learn to take less and less notice of its choices in the future.

2 FIND OUT WHAT YOU REALLY WANT

If you've ever been paralysed in the choice between two courses of action, then you will be pleased to hear that you can use a flip of the coin to find out what you really want to do.

Suppose you are trying to decide whether to spend the evening relaxing at home or attending a party to which some friends have invited you. On the one hand you are feeling tired and would really like to relax for the evening. On the other hand you want to see your friends and meet some new people. You've dithered backwards and forwards, but can't come to a decision.

All you have to do is to flip a coin. The rule is that you have to abide by the result – unless you feel that you want to overrule it. If you do overrule it, then you have discovered which you really wanted to do. If you don't overrule it, then you still have a result you are happy with.

This doesn't break the rule in the previous section about always sticking with the decision of the randomizer. This is because you were doing it with the stated purpose of finding out what you really wanted to do.

3 EXPAND YOUR HORIZONS

Making occasional random choices is a good way of expanding your horizons and having experiences you might not otherwise have.

Here are some suggestions you might try:

1. The next time you are in a restaurant choose what you eat randomly. Obviously if you have a food allergy, then avoid the dishes which might harm you, but otherwise go with the random choice. I've done this often and I've never yet regretted the choice – even when I haven't had the faintest idea what it was!
2. When out for a drive or a walk choose the direction at each junction randomly. You will of course need a passenger in the

car to do the random selection for you, but when walking you can do it yourself.

3 Make a list of six new experiences you might try and choose one of them by throwing a die.

4 Think of some more ways you might use a randomizer and choose one of them randomly.

Putting it all together

This is the reply I sent to someone who wrote to me saying they had a problem with making even simple decisions:

Making decisions is a behaviour which can be learned, just like any other behaviour. You can train yourself to make big decisions by practising making small decisions.

Before you do that, a couple of principles:

1 There are no right or wrong decisions, only decisions with different consequences. You need to train yourself to stop looking for the perfect decision. Instead, your attitude needs to be that you take decisions and deal with the consequences.

2 Doing nothing is a decision in itself. You need to train yourself to think that the choice is not between A and B, but between A, B and C, where C is doing nothing.

Train yourself starting with small things. For example, what are you going to eat for supper tonight? The first choice to make is between: a) having something for supper, and b) having nothing for supper. How are you going to decide which to have? I suggest you flip a coin. That helps you to realize:

1 There is no 'correct' choice

2 That doing nothing is a choice like any other with consequences like any other.

If the 'something for supper' choice comes up, then how do you decide what to eat? Again I suggest you decide entirely at random. Flip a coin, throw dice, whatever. What you are training yourself on here is to recognize that there is no 'correct' choice.

When you've got used to making simple decisions at random, then you can try a slight variation on this. Flip a coin and stick with the answer unless you really want to overrule it. That helps you to identify your own preferences in the matter.

Remember, the aim of this is to practise making decisions. Like any practice, it takes a lot of repetition before the behaviour becomes learned. So don't just do it once or twice and then forget about it. During the day consciously look out for small decisions you can make randomly, and practise it often.

39 EXPERIMENT

All life is an experiment. The more experiments you make the better.
Ralph Waldo Emerson

I would say, as an entrepreneur everything you do – every action you take in product development, in marketing, every conversation you have, everything you do – is an experiment. If you can conceptualize your work not as building features, not as launching campaigns, but as running experiments, you can get radically more done with less effort.
Eric Ries

The biggest job we have is to teach a newly hired employee how to fail intelligently. We have to train him to experiment over and over and to keep on trying and failing until he learns what will work.
Charles Kettering

Children are born true scientists. They spontaneously experiment and experience and re-experience again. They select, combine, and test, seeking to find order in their experiences – 'which is the mostest? which is the leastest?' They smell, taste, bite, and touch-test for hardness, softness, springiness, roughness, smoothness, coldness, warmness: they heft, shake, punch, squeeze, push, crush, rub, and try to pull things apart.
Buckminster Fuller

An expert is a man who has made all the mistakes which can be made in a very narrow field.
Niels Bohr

The productive person doesn't do things just because they have always been done that way. As we've seen, the first characteristic of such a person is a questioning attitude. They ask questions, and then they ask more questions – which have arisen out of the previous questions. They don't just ask questions, but they endeavour to find the answers to them.

After Galileo had asked himself the question 'Do heavy objects fall faster than light objects?', he devised his famous experiment which involved dropping cannon balls of various sizes from the top of the Leaning Tower of Pisa. By doing this experiment, he arrived at the answer 'No, heavy objects do not fall faster than light objects'.

Until someone asked the question everyone had just assumed that heavier objects fell faster. Asking the question opened the way to finding the answer. But the question itself would have achieved nothing unless Galileo had taken action to answer it.

Galileo's asking of the question and his efforts to answer it are typical of the way a productive person works.

1 QUESTIONS SHOULD LEAD TO EXPERIMENTS

The type of experiment you do should fit the type of work you are in. Galileo and Newton were conducting scientific experiments, and scientific experiments require objective measurements resulting from procedures which can be reproduced by other people.

Van Gogh was always experimenting with new ways to paint the world around him, but these were in no sense scientific experiments. They did not produce objectively measurable and reproducible results. The standards he was applying were subjective ones in his own mind, but not any the less real to him and to anyone who appreciates his art.

Henry Ford experimented with industrial processes and with improving the lot of his workers. These were no more scientific experiments than Van Gogh's art was. They were ultimately judged by their success in increasing the profits of his company. Unlike scientific experiments, which can be reproduced for all time, and art, which can be appreciated for as long as it exists, Ford's experiments were probably only valid for his own particular time and society – though many of the lessons learned are still applicable.

You need to be clear in your own mind exactly what sort of experiment you are carrying out. Does it need full scientific rigour, or is it sufficient if it improves your sales? Both these are valid ways of obtaining answers – but only to the right questions.

We have already dealt in Chapter 30 about monitoring key indicators to give us feedback. If you are not a scientist or an artist, but in an ordinary business or leisure situation, monitoring key indicators is the main way of obtaining answers to your experiments.

2 GET IT RIGHT BEFORE YOU INVEST IN IT

The purpose of carrying out experiments is get to the right answer – or perhaps it would be better to say 'get to an answer that works'. Scientific experiments aim to produce one right answer, but for day-to-day living and working there may be many answers that work.

For instance, if you are experimenting with the best way to keep your office tidy, one person will come up with one way of doing it and another person with a different way, but they may both work perfectly satisfactorily. What you are trying to achieve is not some sort of universal perfect answer but a way which is simple, wastes no time and – most important of all – is sustainable. So the key question is 'Does it work?'

The purpose of an experiment is find out what works before you introduce it generally and invest your full time, money and effort into it over the long term.

The methods you discover may continue to be valid for other endeavours even when you have ceased the current one. For instance having written books before I was pretty clear what methods would work for me to get this book written, even though it was quite a few years since I'd written my last one. It was just a matter of once more applying my well-tried routine.

On the other hand, when I decided that I wanted to learn Chinese as a hobby I was not particularly satisfied with the ragbag of methods I had used in the past to achieve my not very brilliant levels in other languages. So I needed to spend some time getting the methodology right. I wanted to develop a daily routine which conformed to the guidelines above – that is to say simple, effective and sustainable. It took me longer than expected because language learning is a field in which there are many different and often contrasting theories about what are the best methods to use. In the end I found a routine which satisfied my criteria. It was worth taking the time to find it because once you have found a routine that works all you have to do is to follow it and progress is virtually inevitable.

3 ALWAYS AIM TO DO BETTER

The productive person approaches the question of how to do something better in two stages. The first is to find a routine or system that works, and the second is to put this into practice until it becomes second nature.

I mentioned in the previous section that I had taken up learning Chinese as a hobby. I was dissatisfied with all my past methods of learning languages so I spent quite a bit of time arriving at a system which was right for me. This was not time wasted because, as one might expect, experimenting with systems to learn Chinese involves learning quite a bit of Chinese along the way. That is in spite of the fact that the methods used aren't optimal. But once I had arrived at a system that worked for me, the way was clear for me to get steadily better and better at Chinese.

You will often hear that Chinese is a very difficult language. The truth is that in itself Chinese is no more difficult than any other language. It just takes an English speaker longer to learn than languages which are closer to English. It's a mistake to think in terms of how difficult any undertaking is. Instead think in terms of how much regular, focused attention it is going to need.

Usually when one person tells another that they need to do better at something what they mean is to work harder and put more effort in. But working harder and putting more effort in is not the way in which a productive person approaches things. The productive person certainly knows that you can't make progress without hard work, but they also know that work comes naturally once you have the right system. So rather than put their attention on psyching themselves up to work harder, they concentrate on developing a better system.

The main characteristic that the best systems share is that they make it easier to do the right thing than the wrong thing.

Putting it all together

To sum up what I have been saying in this chapter, when faced with almost any situation the productive person will follow much the same sequence. It doesn't matter whether they are a scientist, an artist, a manufacturer or a home worker, the sequence is the same.

1. Experiment until you have a process which is simple to work, wastes as little time as possible and is sustainable.
2. Practise the system until it is second nature.

This is contrasted to the unproductive person, who either doesn't have a system at all or puts up with one that doesn't work properly. If they do adopt a new system they don't stick with it long enough to make it second nature, so they end up jumping from one system to another, always looking for the perfect one around the corner which will solve all their problems.

40 LOOK FOR DATA

Experts often possess more data than judgment.
Colin Powell

It is a capital mistake to theorize before one has data.
Sherlock Holmes

Errors using inadequate data are much less than those using no data at all.
Charles Babbage

The greatest deception men suffer is from their own opinions.
Leonardo da Vinci

Prejudice is a great time saver. You can form opinions without having to get the facts.
E. B. White

There is a lot of difference between a judgement firmly founded upon data and a mere opinion. In fact it is impossible to make a judgement without data.

This is unfortunately not the way the world works. People have opinions, which they hold on to firmly in spite of the fact that they are founded on little more than sentiment. Any facts which get in the way of an opinion are ignored. People who hold the opposite opinion are vilified. Since both sides of the argument are working off opinions rather than facts, which side (if either) is right is purely a matter of chance.

It probably doesn't matter too much for most of us if we work off opinions as far as international affairs and politics are concerned because very few of us are likely to be in a position to influence what happens.

But how about your own business?

Do you work off gut feelings, wishful thinking and opinions as far as your own business is concerned? Or are you in full possession of the facts? When you make changes to the way your business is run, are these changes founded on fact or just on theories? Do you follow up rigorously to make sure that the changes are having the intended effect?

Governments are particularly prone to making changes on the basis of unproven theories and then massaging the figures to disguise the disastrous results. Unfortunately what that tells us is that they are more interested in proving themselves right than in finding methods that work. Don't be like them. You are a productive person, who is aiming to make things work – not to protect your own back.

It's also important not to take anything on trust which other people assure you of. Often they will get annoyed or defensive if you ask them to provide figures to back up their assertions. This is usually a very good sign that you were right to ask!

1 WITHOUT DATA YOU HAVE ONLY FEELINGS TO GO ON

In debt counselling one of the first things that the counsellor asks the client to do is to draw up a list of all their debts. This can be something which the client has been avoiding doing through fear. Although they know that they are struggling, they usually have very little idea just how much they are in debt. Indeed they have been deliberately avoiding working out the total.

The result of drawing up this list is almost always that the total turns out to be much larger than the client thought. But paradoxically knowing exactly the extent of their debt brings a sense of relief. Once they have at last faced up to the problem, they can start to draw up a practical plan to deal with it. Previously they were paralysed through fear.

In the field of small businesses, it's surprising how many people will set up a business without making the most elementary calculations about what their sales and profit margins would need to be to make the business a success. I expect you have watched *Dragons' Den* on TV, and you will have seen many people trying to pitch their businesses. It doesn't take many questions from the 'dragons' to establish whether those appearing in front of them have done their homework on their business plans or not.

Data is relevant to a lot more things than money. In fact there are very few fields which you can't express in key numerical indicators. Remember that trends are a lot more informative than single figures. It's certainly useful to know that your credit card debts total £10,000 but it's a lot more useful to know that two years ago they were £5,000, last year they totalled £7,000 and that you're on course for £15,000 in a year's time if you don't do something about it.

2 NEVER TAKE ANYTHING ON TRUST

We've all learned to have a healthy scepticism about politicians' promises and anything said by anyone who is trying to sell us something. What we haven't learned to be sceptical about is anything which accords with our own wishes. We want to be able to afford things, so we ignore all the evidence that we are getting badly into debt. We want our business to be successful so we ignore the evidence that it is not doing well. Above all we want to be right, and we will dismiss or ignore anything that shows we are wrong.

This is a fatal attitude to have if we want to be a productive person. In fact it is one of the key differences between the productive person and the unproductive person:

> The unproductive person decides on their course of action and then finds the evidence that fits what they have already decided.

The productive person looks at the evidence and then decides on their course of action. If new evidence comes up then they revise their course of action.

Before you start thinking that I am recommending the productive person to make decisions based on data only like a computer, remember that one's own feelings are an important part of the evidence. Let's take a look at this in the next section.

3 MAKE SENSE OF THE DATA

At its simplest there are three component parts to the making of a decision. These are:

1. Objective evidence from the real world
2. Our own feelings
3. The decision itself

The difference between making or failing to make a successful decision lies in the order in which these are taken. The order which most textbooks on decision making advise us to follow is:

Gather evidence
Make decision
Feelings

Feelings are actively ignored until after the decision has been made. The theory is that our feelings will automatically come round to support a decision which is objectively good, and provide the motivation needed to implement the decision. Until then they just get in the way of making a good decision.

Another way to make a decision, which I'm sure all of us will recognize, is best known in its manifestation as 'impulse buying'. It goes as follows:

> Feelings
> Make decision
> Gather evidence

The evidence is used to justify the decision, even though the decision was actually made purely from feelings with no reference to the evidence.

The best way to make a decision is actually the following:

> Gather evidence
> Feelings
> Make decision

This is the productive way of making decisions, and is very closely allied with the questioning methods which I described in Chapters 5 and 6. It results in decisions which are both based on fact and in accordance with your feelings on the subject. You are far more likely to be motivated by a decision made this way than by the 'objective' method described by the textbooks. Making a decision without taking feelings into account is likely to lead to a decision which is entirely unsuitable for the reality of the situation.

Putting it all together

Ignoring the data almost always leads either to disaster or to bottling yourself up in your own little bubble in which anything contradicting your opinion is ridiculed or ignored.

To be productive you need to base your work on reality, and the only way to keep aware of reality is to keep in touch with the data. The data of course needs to be of high quality. 'Customer surveys' in which the real aim is to sell people something are not worth the paper they are printed on. Opinion polls suffer from the fact that they are just that – *opinion* polls.

In the business world what counts is what the customer actually does, not what they tell you they are thinking of doing. Comparing the sales results from two test marketings will tell you a lot more than having a focus group tell you which marketing materials they like best. In the world of politics, the odds given by bookies on the results of an election are consistently better at forecasting the result than opinion polls. This is because the odds are based on what people think *will* happen, rather than what they would like to happen.

The principle of obtaining high-quality data can be applied to whatever field you are working in, whether it's paying off your debts, getting people to come to a charity coffee morning, identifying which part of your business is bringing in the most money, or what type of grass grows best on your lawn. All of these and many more are examples of where data is king.

41 SKIM

*He has only half learned the art of reading who has not
added to it the more refined art of skipping and skimming.*
Arthur James Balfour

*A truly great library contains something in
it to offend everyone.*
Jo Goodwin

If you think education is expensive, try ignorance.
Derek Bok

*Some books are to be tasted, others to be swallowed, and
some few are to be chewed and digested.*
Francis Bacon

*I find television very educating. Every time somebody turns on
the set, I go into the other room and read a book.*
Groucho Marx

I'm sure that like most people you have had the experience of
reading a book from beginning to end and then a few months
(or even weeks later) being able to remember practically nothing
of what was in it. Have you ever thumbed through a book in
a book shop, bought it and then found that you got little more
out of reading it than you did while thumbing through it? In
fact most people who have read a book from cover to cover
remember no more about the contents six months later than
someone who has only skimmed through it.

If you are reasonably well acquainted with the subject already
your retention rate will be higher than someone who knew
nothing about it before reading the book. This is because
prior knowledge gives you hooks on which to hang the new

information. How well you retain new information basically depends on how many of these hooks you have already.

If you don't have much prior knowledge of the subject of a book, how can you go about acquiring enough hooks to be able to understand and retain the subject matter? You could try reading a simple introduction to the subject before starting reading a more detailed account. But an equally effective technique is to use the book itself as the source of the hooks by skimming it.

1 SKIMMING GIVES YOU AT LEAST AS MUCH INFORMATION AS READING

Read a book the same way that you read a newspaper. Look at the headlines to see what has happened of interest. Go to your favourite bits and read them. Then read anything that's particularly caught your attention in more detail. Even if you only have a short time available for reading the paper, you will have got the main points of the news. If you have longer you will have more details but the essence is gained very quickly.

I recommend you to get into the habit of skimming books – lots of books. You get far more information from skimming a lot of books quickly than you do from starting out to read one book in detail and then getting stuck – and your retention rate will be better. The ideal place to skim books is in a bookshop or in a library. If you want to go deeper with a particular book you can always buy or borrow it. If you decide that you want to read the whole book from cover to cover, you will have gained a lot of understanding by the preliminary skimming.

2 USE SKIMMING TO IDENTIFY WHERE YOU WANT TO GO DEEPER

Skimming will help you to identify the parts of the book which you want to read more closely. Many books keep the kernel of their message in one or two chapters, so you can then skip the padding and go straight to the message. With a text book you may only be interested in certain aspects of the subject, so again you can identify where those parts are by skimming.

The chapter headings and table of contents are a great help in this. But don't forget the book's index. For instance, if you are interested in the life of the poet John Keats, you can read the passages about him in multiple books about poetry in general or the historical period by looking up the references to him in their indexes.

3 WHEN YOU WRITE MAKE IT EASY TO SKIM

You can make it easy for people to skim your own writings by using the same format as a newspaper article. First you have the headline, which should give the gist in as few words as possible. The first paragraph summarizes the contents. This is followed by the detail of the story. The skimmer can see from the headline whether the story is likely to be at all relevant. Then they have the choice of just reading the first paragraph to get the summary, or going on to read the main article.

NEVERLAND CHILD IN POISONOUS SPIDER SCARE

A ten-year-old girl, daughter of Neverland residents Marvin and Jeanne Muffet, escaped unharmed on Thursday when a poisonous spider landed next to her while she was eating her lunch outdoors.

Neverland Police have confirmed that the first incident of the giant 'fairytale' spider being seen in the Neverland area occurred on Thursday when a child narrowly escaped being bitten. Jeanne Muffet said that her daughter was sitting on a tuffet eating her curds and whey when...

Whatever you are writing – a report, article, blog post, chapters in a text book, email – make it easy for the skimmer. Remember – headline, summary, full story.

It's not only skimmers that it makes it easier for either. It makes your writing more comprehensible to the people who want to read it all. The headline and summary paragraph give them hooks on which they can hang the details of the story as they progress through the article or chapter.

Putting it all together

Skimming is a bit of an art form. Most people develop their own techniques to suit their own preferred style. If you haven't yet developed a technique that you are happy with, then identify an area in which you are already using skimming and apply the way you are doing it to other forms of reading. People are usually most familiar with skimming books in a bookshop, or magazines in a newsagent. For serious skimming, it can help if you think of the chapters in a book as a series of magazines laid out on a shelf.

Skimming is unfortunately still one area in which printed books are greatly superior to electronic books. It's very difficult to skim an electronic book effectively, though there have been some developments lately in e-reader software which are intended to make it easier.

If you need to revise an article or book that you've already read from end to end, then try reverse skimming. Don't re-read it completely again – at least to start with – but skim it and allow your mind to refresh its memory of the contents.

Even re-skimming a book that you've done nothing more than skim in the past can be very effective. During the passage of time your understanding of the subject and its context will have deepened, and you may well find that you get much more out of it than when you first skimmed it.

Maybe you're one of those people who knows the first few pages of hundreds of books virtually off by heart because you keep re-starting the book from the beginning. If so you will find that skimming is the answer because it encourages you to take on a book as a whole in any order.

PRODUCTIVITY IN ACTION

So far I have written in general terms about productivity, what it consists of, the productive attitude and productive work. In this section I shall be dealing with how the productive person can apply these principles in specific situations.

42 PRODUCTIVE WRITING

Easy reading is damn hard writing.
Nathaniel Hawthorne

There are three rules for writing a novel. Unfortunately, no one knows what they are.
W. Somerset Maugham

I love deadlines. I love the whooshing noise they make as they go by.
Douglas Adams

You never have to change anything you got up in the middle of the night to write.
Saul Bellow

Being a writer is a very peculiar sort of a job: it's always you versus a blank sheet of paper (or a blank screen) and quite often the blank piece of paper wins.
Neil Gaiman

In one form or another most of us have to do quite a bit of writing, and there are few people who find it easy even when the subject is one which excites and motivates them. A lot of subjects are far from exciting and motivating – essays, theses, reports, newspaper and magazine articles are a few that spring to mind – yet they still have to be written. The ability to write reliably to meet a deadline is a valuable skill.

For this chapter I interviewed Andreas Eschbach, a prolific and very popular writer of thrillers in German. He is not very well known outside German-speaking countries although some of his books, such as *A Trillion Dollars*, have been published in English. He is a good example though of an author who writes a large number of books in a systematic way.

1 WRITING AND EDITING ARE TWO SEPARATE PROCESSES

Do you complete your research for a book before starting the writing process?

I always try to, but in the writing I invariably stumble upon a lot of open questions. I don't let them stop me, I put placeholders in the text (or use comment functions, if available) and continue writing, leaving the research of these details for later.

It looks like: 'He pulled out his +NAME OF PISTOL+ and aimed it at his opponent.'

This concerns however only minor details which I want to include to enhance the realism of the text. The big issues – those that determine whether a plot idea will work or not – have to be researched thoroughly before typing the first sentence of the novel.

Do you edit as you go along or leave that to last?

With one exception, which I will explain in a second, I don't edit while writing the first draft. I even try not to read what I have until everything is written down.

I was unsure about this for a long time. I always had the feeling that reading my work in progress could easily unsettle, demotivate or even derail me, so I avoided it, although I felt guilty about it. Then I read an interview with Nadine Gordimer where she explained that she did exactly the same – only read the whole thing once the first draft was finished. I was relieved. If it's good enough for a Nobel laureate, it's surely good enough for me.

2 HAVE A DAILY ROUTINE FOR WRITING

Do you have a daily routine for writing? How do you fit it in with all the other stuff you have to do?

On a normal day, the morning belongs to the novel, the afternoon to everything else. This means that after lunch, I pull out my task list, enter the task 'write novel' at the end and process from there. So it's always an option to simply continue writing.

My starter routine in the morning is (this is the exception I just mentioned) to read the last two pages I've written the day before and edit any faults or weaknesses I find. However, it's not the editing that's important, but the fact that doing so puts me back into the story and into 'writing mode'.

How do you ensure that you meet the deadline for the delivery of the book to the publisher? Do you keep track of your word count or do you have some other way of doing it?

Yes, I keep track of my word count. Every month I print out a calendar sheet and set word targets for every weekday. This looks a little crazy, but I have to do it because I am basically a lazy person. I need to see whether I'm ahead of plan or behind, so every evening I note the word count and the difference from the target and feel good if I'm ahead. This routine keeps me on travel speed – it's like running against myself (Saturday and Sunday are buffers to catch up if I have to).

Unfortunately, this doesn't prevent me from falling back seriously if I get stuck on an unforeseen story problem which has to be solved before I can continue. When that happens I simply print a new sheet, adjust the word targets and cancel a few appointments to catch up. Over the years, I have gained the experience to know how much buffer time I need in order not to be forced to call the publisher for a later deadline.

3 USE QUESTIONING TO KEEP THE FLOW GOING

Do you have any top tips for avoiding 'writer's block'.

First, you have to look closer at what's stopping you from writing.

The main reasons when the 'flow' stops are:

1. You don't know exactly how the story has to continue. Remedy: Take a long walk and think it through. Or have an evening with a pen and a notebook in solitude. Or discuss the case with a confidant.
2. You have lost the inner connection to your story. Remedy: Try to remember why you wanted to write in the first place. Why it was important? What if you were to die without having written this story?
3. Fear. Fear of writing badly. Inner editor lurking over your inner shoulder, criticizing ceaselessly Every. Single. Word. You. Write. Remedy: Write as fast and as ugly as possible. Make the window of your word processor so small that you can only see the last two words, and then write for at least twenty minutes without stopping for more than three seconds. Blow the block out. This works wonders and is absolutely worth a few bleeding fingertips!
4. Tiredness. Bodily exhaustion. Remedy: Have a break. Do something else. Get enough sleep.

Important: Only if one identifies the real reason can one determine the appropriate cure. Having a break will not help if the problem is not knowing how to continue, speedwriting will not cure tiredness, and so on.

Even more important: Every novel-writing project reaches a low point eventually, a point when one hates the damned thing and wishes one had started with another idea in the first place. A point where one really runs against a wall. But this is a normal, unavoidable part of the creation process. This is when the novel transforms the writer and teaches him an important lesson.

Nothing is wrong with having some periods of struggle. They will pass, and they don't mean you lack talent. It's the talentless writers who never question their writing.

Putting it all together

Most writers agree that the secret to producing output, whether it's a short article or blog post or a complete novel, is to concentrate on writing the first draft without worrying about its quality. To get this draft finished, they will use routines. The most important thing about a routine is that you stick to it.

Once the first draft is finished comes the editing. Writing and editing must be seen as two separate processes. Again it's important to develop routines to cover the editing process.

The routines that Andreas has described in the interview above work for him, but they don't have to be the same routines that you use. His routines are a good starting point, but what is important is that you develop routines that suit your style and work for you.

43 PRODUCTIVE TEAMWORK

If everyone is moving forward together, then success takes care of itself.
Henry Ford

Teamwork is the ability to work together toward a common vision. The ability to direct individual accomplishments toward organizational objectives. It is the fuel that allows common people to attain uncommon results.
Andrew Carnegie

Alone we can do so little; together we can do so much.
Helen Keller

The strength of the team is each individual member. The strength of each member is the team.
Phil Jackson

If two men on the same job agree all the time, then one is useless. If they disagree all the time, both are useless.
Darryl F. Zanuck

Teams come in all sorts of shapes and sizes. There are hierarchical teams with a clearly defined pecking order, with one person acting as leader and working to laid down terms of reference. There are informal teams of equals who meet with no particular procedure. There are partnerships between two or more people. And many others. You may find yourself a member of several teams at once, each of a different nature. You may be the leader, an equal partner or one of the subordinates. You may have a clearly defined role within the team or you may not.

Teams exist in order to arrive at a certain goal. At least that's the theory, but unfortunately some teams continue to exist long after their usefulness has been exhausted. If you find yourself wondering what purpose you serve by being on a particular team, then the answer is that you shouldn't be on it – and you should make every effort to be removed from it.

If you are setting up a team or a partnership, resist the temptation to recruit people exactly like yourself. Remember that the strength of a good team comes from the varied experience and abilities of its members. So the people you recruit should have complementary skills not identical skills.

1 RETAIN OWNERSHIP OF THE PROJECT

Whatever your position in a team, whether you are the team leader or not, as a productive person you need to establish in your own mind a sense of ownership over the team's work. This means that you must see it as your responsibility to bring the team to arrive at its goal. If all the members of the team have this sense of ownership the team will thrive.

This attitude is more than just being cooperative. It means that in some sense you must see it as your responsibility to lead the team towards a successful conclusion to the project.

In particular you must use a questioning attitude both about the goal of the team and about the team's processes as well. The correct functioning of a team is more about setting up the right processes than about anything else. You need to help the team do this. (Chapter 4 is a good reference to keep in mind.)

Remember above all that a process is judged by its results, and that if the results currently being produced by the team are not satisfactory that is because their processes are not properly designed to produce the right results.

2 SCHEDULING IS THE KEY

The working of a team depends on successful processes which are designed to produce the right results. But what are the right results?

The ultimate purpose of a team is to produce the schedules from which a project will be run. It is the quality of these schedules which will decide whether the project will turn out to be successful or not. Project control is fundamentally about ensuring that the schedules are adhered to and kept under evaluation so that they are amended as necessary.

This applies whether you are planning the next outing of your local senior citizens' club, a fundraising campaign for the church spire, or a new motorway network for the North of England. The principles are the same, only the scale is different.

For major industrial and commercial projects there are many sophisticated project planning methods. This book is not intended to be a project planning manual, so I do not intend to go into any of these. But however simple or sophisticated a project schedule is, its purpose is to enable a group of people to work together to produce a defined result within a certain period. It is the schedule which keeps them all working together in a co-ordinated fashion.

3 THE TEAM PROCESS

As I mentioned above, process is at the heart of team work. Even in the relatively informal setting of two people working together on a small project, leaving processes undefined will result in mistakes being made, essential actions missed, continual unnecessary emergencies and misunderstandings. Failure to define the processes at the earliest stage will inevitably lead to problems down the road.

You therefore need to start with a questioning stage. Here are some of the typical questions which need to be considered:

What are the essential procedures that we need to establish in order to plan this project?
Who does what?
What processes need to be set up?

How do we report back to each other?

How do we resolve disputes?

What else do we need to agree?

Putting it all together

Teams have a natural tendency to lose focus and coordination if not carefully controlled. So working out exactly how that control is to be exercised is a high priority right at the start.

Like all the subjects in this section of the book, working as part of a team can be made much more productive by the use of the productivity principles – a questioning attitude leading to the setting up of processes. By encouraging your fellow team members to use the same principles many of the common problems with teams can be avoided.

A productive team can be the means by which a productive person extends the influence of their thinking and action far beyond what they could achieve on their own.

44 PRODUCTIVE EXERCISING

True enjoyment comes from activity of the mind and exercise of the body; the two are ever united.
Wilhelm von Humboldt

Leave all the afternoon for exercise and recreation, which are as necessary as reading. I will rather say more necessary because health is worth more than learning.
Thomas Jefferson

Look at our society. Everyone wants to be thin, but nobody wants to diet. Everyone wants to live long, but few will exercise. Everybody wants money, yet seldom will anyone budget or control their spending.
John C. Maxwell

Those who think they have not time for bodily exercise will sooner or later have to find time for illness.
Edward Stanley

I see exercise taking this perverted detour. The original intention of exercise was to heal and maintain health. Now I see it as having nothing to do with health. I see most exercises based on looking good. They actually make you less healthy. You overdevelop the obvious muscles. You take drugs to enhance that. You ignore the rest, and you become more out of balance.
Bryan Kest

We seem to be always reading about how beneficial exercise is to health. This is of course true. Without exercise it is impossible to be at peak productivity. People who do primarily mental work can easily forget that their brains are part of their bodies and, like any other part of our bodies, are influenced by everything that happens to the body.

But there is a negative side to this stress on exercise. For some reason it is easy to get obsessed about it. Exercising is very subject to fashion and, as Bryan Kest says above, often the goal of 'being healthy' becomes subordinated to 'looking good'.

For the productive person exercise is an essential part of life, which like every other part of life is seen as a field in which the rules of productivity have sway. The first rule of productivity is to question, the second to establish good processes.

1 BE CLEAR ABOUT YOUR AIM

The first and most important question to ask about exercise is 'What do I want to achieve by exercising?'

Everything that you decide to do about exercise depends on your answer to this question. Without asking it, you may find yourself exercising in an inappropriate way which makes it difficult for you to keep going for the long ride – and the long ride is always the only way to exercise successfully. Lack of clarity about your reasons for exercising means a lack of consistent motivation. Lack of consistent motivation usually means starting with a great burst of enthusiasm and then giving up after a few weeks.

Here are some possible reasons why you might want to exercise:

> Olympic gold medal
> Fitness for leisure sports
> General health
> Looking good

Looking at this list it's very clear that these possible reasons would require very different levels of commitment and type of exercise. They would also take vastly different amounts of time.

Whatever you decide your own personal reasons for exercising are, the next step is to set up good processes to achieve them.

Spending time to get these right is going to mean the difference between failure and success.

2 GET THE PROCESS CLEAR

It is a big mistake to fail to establish an exercise regime which you can keep to. This is true whether your aim is Olympic gold or exercise for general health purposes. The principle is the same – it is just a matter of degree.

Relying on willpower alone is never enough. A well-designed routine is one which is easy to keep to – ideally even easier than not keeping to it. Use the Productivity Time Management System (Chapter 9) and personal average monitoring (Chapter 36) as elements of your plan. Personal average monitoring is particularly important because it is highly motivating to see that you are making constant improvement.

3 DON'T CONFUSE HEALTH AND FITNESS

Being healthy and being fit are two different things. By its very nature exercise puts a strain on the body, and pushing yourself too far too soon is asking for trouble. Don't ignore warning signs of injury either. The history of sport is full of examples of people damaging their health in the pursuit of fitness.

Be sure to aim to beat your personal average rather than your personal best each session. You will be much less likely to cause yourself injury because when you aim to beat your personal average you are aiming at something which is well within your capabilities. On the other hand, when you aim to beat your personal best you are continually pushing yourself into territory which your body hasn't yet learned to cope with.

Putting it all together

For many people an exercise programme starts in a burst of enthusiasm and then fizzles out after a few weeks. We may spend a great deal of money and time buying the latest bits of kit, taking out gym subscriptions and reading books and magazine articles about exercising. In the midst of all this activity, not a great deal of exercising actually gets done.

The productive person tackles the setting up of an exercise programme in a different way. First they ask the necessary questions to establish exactly why they want to exercise, what the best form of exercise is for their aims and the amount of time they have available, and what resources they need.

After that the next step is to design an exercise routine which they can easily keep to. The aim of the routine is as far as possible to make it easier to exercise than not to exercise so that there is minimal dependence on willpower. One of the most essential parts of the routine is careful monitoring of the results because as improvement is seen so motivation grows.

45 PRODUCTIVE DIETING

A culture fixated on female thinness is not an obsession about female beauty, but an obsession about female obedience. Dieting is the most potent political sedative in women's history; a quietly mad population is a tractable one.
Naomi Wolf

No one wakes up in the morning and says, 'I want to gain 150 pounds and I will start right now!'
Tricia Cunningham

Food is an important part of a balanced diet.
Frances Ann Lebowitz

Weight and body oppression is oppressive to everyone. When you live in a society that says that one kind of body is bad and another is good, those with 'good' bodies constantly fear that their bodies will go 'bad', and those with 'bad' bodies are expected to feel shame and do everything they can to have 'good' bodies. In the process, we torture our bodies, and do everything from engage in disordered eating to invasive surgery to make ourselves okay. Nobody wins in this kind of struggle.
Golda Poretsky

That eating should be foremost about bodily health is a relatively new and, I think, destructive idea – destructive not just the pleasure of eating, which would be bad enough, but paradoxically of our health as well. Indeed, no people on earth worry more about the health consequences of their food choices than we Americans – and no people suffer from as many diet-related problems. We are becoming a nation of orthorexics: people with an unhealthy obsession with healthy eating.
Michael Pollan

Diet and exercise go closely together and most of what I have said in the previous chapter applies to dieting – only more so.

Perhaps there is more conflicting advice about dieting than about any other subject – it certainly feels like it – to the extent that the ordinary person finds it almost impossible to identify what is sound advice and what isn't. Here I want to make the disclaimer that I'm certainly not qualified to give advice on dieting as such. That is why in this chapter I will confine myself to looking at how a productive person might approach the subject.

So how would a productive person approach a minefield like this? As I said in the previous chapter on the subject of exercise, the first rule of productivity is to question, the second to establish good processes. How might we do this in the context of dieting?

1 ASK QUESTIONS ABOUT DIETING

The first thing to establish is why you want to diet. Since dieting is even more tied up with self-image than exercising is, it is worth spending some time on this question and any questions which flow from it. Rather than just trying to give your reasons off the top of your head, use some of the questioning techniques given in Chapters 5 and 6. I would particularly recommend repeating the question 'What are my five best ideas for what I want to achieve by dieting?' over five days or so, as described in Chapter 6. This is a particularly good question for digging down to deeper motivation.

Once you've become clear about your reasons for dieting, it's time to establish what results you want. At this stage you can start to design a process for yourself to follow.

2 ESTABLISH A PROCESS FOR DIETING

It's generally agreed that dieting goes hand in hand with exercise, so you will probably want to design processes for both at the same time.

Whatever processes you decide on, the key to their success will be in the monitoring of the results. This monitoring provides both direction and motivation. For exercise, the data to monitor will be such things as distance, number of repetitions, speed and duration among others. But what sort of data should we be monitoring for dieting?

The most obvious is weight. Although to a certain extent weight naturally varies on a daily basis, it is easiest to monitor it *as if* the daily weight reading were meaningful. Over a few days the natural variations will even out.

Other possible measures are body measurements on a weekly or monthly basis, or the number of calories eaten each day. Whatever measure or measures you choose, monitor them using the personal average method described in Chapter 36.

But of course there are many reasons for dieting other than weight loss. As an exercise, think about what data you would monitor if *you* were to go on a diet. To answer the question, you will need to be clear about what you would be hoping to achieve through dieting.

3 DON'T BE OBSESSIVE

Dieting is an activity which can easily tip over into obsession. The best shield against this is clarity about one's aims. So don't neglect the need for questioning your aims in a non-superficial way, as outlined in the first section of this chapter. As well as guarding you against becoming obsessive it will also give you motivation not to give up after you have got over the initial burst of enthusiasm.

Another guard against obsession is the technique of trying to beat your personal average rather than your personal best. Doing this will stop you from pushing yourself further and faster than your body is capable of dealing with. It will also help you to level off and maintain your results once you have achieved your aim.

Putting it all together

Dieting is a notoriously difficult field in which there are a huge number of pitfalls. It is closely associated with exercise, which shares many of its pitfalls. Both are very strongly tied up with notions of body image. However both exercise and diet can hardly be avoided if one is to lead a healthy lifestyle.

The productive person's best defences against the dangers of both diet and exercise is to be very clear about what their objectives are and to set up good processes to achieve these objectives.

46 PRODUCTIVE FRIENDSHIP

Be slow to fall into friendship; but when thou art in,
continue firm and constant.

Socrates

My best friend is the one who brings out the best in me.

Henry Ford

True friendship comes when the silence between
two people is comfortable.

David Tyson Gentry

True friendship is when you walk into their house and your
WiFi connects automatically.

Anon

Love is like the wild-rose briar;
Friendship is like the holly-tree.
The holly is dark when the rose briar blooms,
But which will bloom most constantly?

Emily Brontë

It's surprising with an important subject like friendship how little there is written about it these days. Magazines and books are full of advice about 'love', but friendship seems to be one of those subjects in which people are left to their own devices most of the time. Yet there are few people who would claim that their friendships are in really good order. Unfortunately asking for help over friendship seems to be the equivalent of admitting that one has no friends, and no one wants to admit that.

Friendship can be a source of great depth and consolation in life, but it (or the lack of it) can also be the source of some of life's greatest sadnesses. Maybe it seems strange to ask what the purpose of friendship in general is – and even stranger to ask what the purpose of a particular friendship is. Yet these are the sort of questions that need answering before one can approach friendship in a productive manner.

The productive person approaches friendship first and foremost by being clear about what they want out of a friendship. And, as you might suspect, the productive person is systematic about how they go about friendship, particularly the maintenance of individual friendships.

1 FRIENDSHIPS NEED SUFFICIENT REGULAR FOCUSED ATTENTION LIKE ANY OTHER SUBJECT

The secret to initiating and maintaining friendships is not very difficult. In fact it's the same as for every other subject that the productive person is involved in. What is needed is sufficient, regular, focused attention.

A good friendship is rather like a plant. It needs watering at regular intervals. Also like a plant, it doesn't respond well to being overwatered, that is to say drowned in too much attention.

This all sounds very obvious, but how many friendships have 'cooled' on you because you neglected to keep in regular contact? If you ask yourself the question why you neglected to keep in regular contact, the answer may be that for one reason or another you decided to let the friendship lapse. That's your decision and is absolutely fine. But the answer might also be that you just didn't get around to it. And why didn't you get around to it? Because you aren't systematic about maintaining your friendships.

The good news is that a friendship that has lapsed can often be revived simply by paying attention to it again. A friendship can remain dormant for years, and then some chance contact or an email out of the blue can revive it again.

2 THE BEST WAY TO MAINTAIN FRIENDSHIPS IS TO MAINTAIN THE SUBJECT AROUND WHICH THEY WERE FORMED

By and large friendships never get formed in a vacuum. At the beginning they usually centre around some subject. Some typical reasons for the start of a friendship would include:

You are at school or university together

Your children are at school together

You are neighbours

You are work colleagues

You belong to the same club, association or church

This list is of course nowhere near exhaustive. It doesn't include one of the most important and durable reasons for a close friendship:

You are related

The tendency is for friendships to wither once the original reason for their existence disappears. If you maintain the subject around which the friendship formed your chances of maintaining the friendship are greatly increased. How might you do this? Typical ways are to organize reunions, attend events, keep links going and correspond about shared interests. If you are friends with someone you are related to then paying attention to the *whole* family will help to cement your friendship with one or more individual family members.

3 FRIENDSHIPS TAKE TIME SO THERE IS A LIMIT TO THE NUMBER OF EFFECTIVE FRIENDSHIPS

It actually takes quite a bit of work to maintain a friendship, especially if the situation or location where the friendship was formed no longer applies. Therefore it makes sense to limit the number of people with whom you wish to maintain a real friendship. You simply don't have time to carry out the sort of actions I mentioned at the end of the previous section for more than a carefully selected number of people.

That doesn't mean you can't have plenty of acquaintances. The real difference between an acquaintance and a friend is that you don't need to maintain acquaintances. People will come in and out of your life and you can maintain perfectly friendly relations with them without making them into real friends.

The difference between an acquaintance and a friend:

Acquaintance: 'We really must get together sometime this year.'
Friend: 'Let's fix a date to get together. Have you got your diary with you?'

As always, the productive person seeks clarity before acting. So they need to ask questions about what exactly an effective friendship would consist of with a particular person, and what it is that they would want to get out of the friendship. In the light of their answers, they then need to decide how the friendship should be conducted.

Putting it all together

It may sound very cold-blooded to plan one's friendships in the way I have outlined, but the alternative is to have unsatisfactory friendships which never reach their full potential. Bringing clarity and system to friendships means that one can make the most of one's opportunities for friendship – which in many people's lives are few and far between. As Socrates said, as quoted at the start of this chapter, 'Be slow to fall into friendship; but when thou art in, continue firm and constant.'

I hope you are beginning to get the idea that there are no areas of life to which a productive person can't bring the principles of productivity. Any areas which they don't bring these principles to are likely to be unsatisfactory and not measure up to the high standards of the rest of their life. It would be a pity if friendship were to be one of these because of the great value that it can bring to our lives.

47 PRODUCTIVE CHILD-REARING

*There's nothing that can help you understand your beliefs
more than trying to explain them to an inquisitive child.*
Frank A. Clark

*It's not what you do for your children, but what you have
taught them to do for themselves, that will make them
successful human beings.*
Ann Landers

*The natural state of motherhood is unselfishness. When you
become a mother, you are no longer the centre of your own
universe. You relinquish that position to your children.*
Jessica Lange

*While we try to teach our children all about life, our children
teach us what life is all about.*
Angela Schwindt

*When it comes to developing character strength, inner security
and unique personal and interpersonal talents and skills in a
child, no institution can or ever will compare with, or effectively
substitute for, the home's potential for positive influence.*
Stephen Covey

Bringing up children is one of the most challenging and
rewarding things that we can do as adults. As productive
people we want to make the most of this time, both to give our
children a fine start in life and also in the process to develop as
human beings ourselves. Hence there are two main aspects to
child-rearing to which productive people need to pay attention.
The first is to use the productivity principles for our own
understanding and practice of child-rearing. The second is to
teach the principles of productivity to our children by example
and explanation.

1 QUESTION YOUR OWN PRACTICE OF CHILD-REARING

Like any other situation or project, child-rearing needs thought and consideration for it to be successful. Therefore make it the subject of questioning and continuous feed back. Bringing up children is a tremendous challenge for a couple, and an even greater challenge for one person on their own. With a couple there may be tensions which require sorting out, and asking the right questions can be essential. And the same is true for a single parent, particularly if they don't have a great deal of support.

The sort of questions that you might ask include:

> What do I want for my children?
>
> What do I want to get out of bringing my children up?
>
> What sort of support do I need?
>
> What are the best things I can do to help my children?
>
> What are the most fun things that we can do together as a family?

I'm sure you can think of many more.

2 ENCOURAGE YOUR CHILDREN TO ASK QUESTIONS

Most parents dread their children's questions, but in fact we should encourage them – and help them to answer them themselves as far as possible. Questioning comes very naturally when children are at a certain age and it's a great time for them to learn, and even more important learn how to learn.

Unfortunately rather than use and build on their children's questions, many parents try to squash them because they find the incessant stream of 'Why's' too much to handle. But in fact you can stop your children's questions getting on your nerves by joining in and even anticipating their questions by asking things like 'Why do you think that I'm doing this?', 'Do you know what that animal is called?' and so on.

3 ENCOURAGE YOUR CHILDREN IN GOOD PROCESS

As well as encouraging your children's questioning powers, you can also teach them the importance of good processes. My wife for instance is an extremely good organizer of family events, and she still uses the methods which were taught to her by her mother when she was a child. That says a lot about how her mother took every opportunity to involve her in what she was doing and encouraged her to try things out for herself.

Children need to see what the purpose of a routine or process is and to be involved in the decisions about what the process should be. In that way their interest is stimulated and they don't feel that they are being forced to do something they don't want to do.

Encourage them to apply good processes to the things they themselves want to do, not just the things you want them to do!

Putting it all together

I've included chapters on 'personal' subjects like exercise, dieting, friendship and child-rearing because I wanted to make the point that productivity is not just something that applies to the world of work. Truly productive people aren't just productive in one part of their lives – they are productive in their whole lives. There is a tendency to compartmentalize one's life so that the methods that work in one part of one's life are not used to improve the other parts. Van Gogh for example was highly productive when it came to his art, but the rest of his life was a disaster.

A better example would be that of the brothers John and Charles Wesley who transformed the spiritual life of their country in the eighteenth century by being as methodical about their religion as other people were about their businesses, hence the name 'Methodists' – which was originally intended as an insult. Where did the Wesleys get their methodical approach? It was instilled into them virtually from the cradle by their parents Samuel and Susanna Wesley.

48 PRODUCTIVE FINANCES

Money won't create success, the freedom to make it will.
Nelson Mandela

The hardest thing to understand in the world is the income tax.
Albert Einstein

Sometimes your best investments are the ones you don't make.
Donald Trump

Money can't buy love but it improves your bargaining position.
Anon

Ben Franklin may have discovered electricity – but it is the man who invented the meter who made the money.
Earl Warren

In the last few chapters we have been looking at ways in which the principles of productivity can be applied in various common life situations: writing, teamwork, exercise, dieting, friendship and bringing up children. These are all areas which many people find difficult, but of course there are many others. The point is that the principles of productivity can be applied in any situation. So in this chapter I am going to be looking at another area which causes difficulty to many people, that of finances.

I have no intention of writing an investment manual, which I'm certainly not qualified to do. All I want to achieve is to show that our personal and business finances are something which responds to the productive mind-set just as much as anything else does.

So I am going to treat this chapter as an exercise in which you can practise applying the principles for yourself.

How might you apply these principles? Let's have a look. I suggest that you actually work through the questions and instructions, regardless of whether you feel that your finances need attention. It will be good practice because this is the procedure that you can use for any subject or sphere of action.

1 QUESTIONING

Money is usually considered such an obviously good thing to have, that most people rarely ask themselves any questions about why they want it. Yet it's very necessary to do so if you want to have a healthy attitude to your work, your spending and your saving.

So decide what questions you would want to ask yourself about money, and how you would go about asking yourself those questions. Remember the principles and techniques given in Chapters 5 and 6 and decide the best way to go about this.

2 PROCESSES AND ROUTINES

Having answered the questions – though this should be a continuing process – the next stage is to set up processes and routines, both business and personal.

Think what sort of routines you would need in order to run your finances successfully. Can you automate any of them? What do you need to do yourself, and what can you get other people to do for you?

Remember, having good processes and routines is what will set you apart from the majority of people. It's difficult to be productive on a consistent basis without them.

3 CONSTANT FEEDBACK

Having set up your processes and routines, it's vitally important to know exactly where you are on a daily or weekly basis. You don't want to be like my example in Chapter 30 of a company owner trying to run his business off the quarterly balance sheet.

One of the most common mistakes I see people make is that when their income expands they expand their lifestyle to match. This has several adverse results. First you will be making little in the way of savings. Second you will be giving yourself no reserve or margin for error. And third you will have to keep working hard to keep your income at the same level. A bad month or two or an unexpected illness and you will find yourself struggling to keep up.

So, what key indicators do you need to monitor to ensure that your finances are heading in the right direction? How are you going to do this?

See if you can work out the answers to these questions for your own circumstances.

Putting it all together

Do you know what your current personal liquid assets are at this precise date? If you don't, as an exercise write down an estimated figure. Then work out what the correct figure is. How accurate was your estimate?

A further question: are your liquid assets getting larger or smaller? If you don't know, how can you find out?

A person who is being productive in all areas of their life will have these answers at their fingertips. They have to, because you can't be productive if you don't have this sort of information.

The way I have outlined for your finances is the basic template for bringing productivity to any field of endeavour. Finances are a good place to start because often you can see an improvement very quickly. Once you've got the hang of how the principles work you can apply them wherever you feel they are needed.

49 PRODUCTIVE LIVING TO THE MAXIMUM

Carpe diem! Rejoice while you are alive; enjoy the day;
live life to the fullest; make the most of what you have.
It is later than you think.

Horace

It is nothing to die. It is frightful not to live.

Victor Hugo

The patterns are simple, but followed together, they make
for a whole that is wiser than the sum of its parts. Go for a
walk; cultivate hunches; write everything down, but keep your
folders messy; embrace serendipity; make generative mistakes;
take on multiple hobbies; frequent coffeehouses and other
liquid networks; follow the links; let others build on your ideas;
borrow, recycle; reinvent. Build a tangled bank.

Steven Johnson

Always be a first-rate version of yourself, instead of a second-
rate version of somebody else.

Judy Garland

It is not where we are that matters nor what we have, it is
what we do with where we are and what we have.

Sonia Rumzi

Living to the maximum involves being able to trust yourself to
get things done. If you can't trust yourself for that then you are
never going to be successful in your own eyes.

What is the biggest constraint on a productive person who
wishes to live life to the maximum? The answer is time. The most
productive and the least productive people share one thing in

common. They are both issued with twenty-four hours of time each day from the day they were born to the day that they die. What counts is what they do with that time. It's not what they intended to do in the future, or what they might have got round to doing sometime. It's what they actually do each day.

That's why I don't recommend to-do lists. Lists take you into the realm of make-believe, a dream country which will never exist or which will already be outdated by the time you get there.

1 FIND OUT WHAT YOU REALLY WANT TO DO

Living to the maximum means different things to different people, but in general it means being able to carry through on what you really want to do. So it's surprising how few people are clear about where they'd like to see their lives going – whether in the short-term or the long-term. And even fewer people are actually doing what in their best dreams they would want to be doing.

The place to start then is to identify what you really want to do. The simple question 'What are the five things I most want to do?' asked for five days in a row will bring a lot of clarity into your life. This exercise that should be repeated at least three or four times a year. (See Chapter 6 for more details on how to do this exercise.)

Doing what you really want to do is of course not just a matter of being clear about what you want. You also need to have the motivation and ability to carry it out. Fortunately a characteristic of this type of questioning exercise is that as you answer the question each day some of the answers will start to take on a life of their own and you will feel the energy to get moving on them. So doing this exercise results not only in answers to the question but often also the motivation to put them into action.

2 TRAIN YOURSELF TO BE PRODUCTIVE

The most basic routine to establish in your life as a productive person is your time management system. Getting this particular low-level process right goes a long way towards freeing you up for higher-level productive work. Remember that, as with any low-level system, you shouldn't need to think about it more than necessary. If you are continually fiddling around with the system, then you are paying more attention to the system than you are to getting the work done.

One of the advantages of the type of time management system I am advocating – one that doesn't depend on a to-do list – is that at the end of each day you end up with a list of everything that you have actually *done* during your discretionary time. It is good practice at the end of the day to check through the list and ask yourself such questions as: 'Is this what I want to spend my time on?', 'What should I have done which I didn't?' and 'What would I have been better off not doing?'

As well as showing what you have done, the list also shows you the amount you are *capable of doing* during a single day. So if you decide that you should have done some things which you didn't do, you also need to identify the tasks you would have left undone in order to make room for them.

3 ABOVE ALL BE PERSISTENT

As I've stressed repeatedly, the productive techniques in this book are generally low-level, but it's essential to get the low-level processes right if you are going to be able to control the high-level stuff.

If you fail to establish good low-level processes, or keep chopping and changing them – or worse, giving up on them – you will achieve far less than your potential. Persistence is essential to real achievement.

One of your greatest aids to persistence is the recommended time-management system. A 'no-list' system like the one described in this book encourages persistency because it concentrates on building on a solid foundation of what you *have* done, rather than constantly chasing the will-o'-the-wisp of what you *might* do in the future. To-do lists have a tendency to encourage continual diversification, spreading what one is trying to do thinner and thinner until one is just dabbling at countless projects and getting none of them done properly.

Putting it all together

If you've taken one message away from this book it should be that both 'being positive' and 'being negative' are blind alleys that lead nowhere. Success does not come from sitting around trying to get into the right frame of mind – it comes from engaging with the project and working with it. Positive feelings will naturally emerge from doing this.

Rather than having a positive or negative attitude, the key-word is to be *realistic*. You will find problems and set-backs much easier to deal with if you simply take a realistic attitude to them. Be clear what is needed to be done, be clear what you can do, and be clear about your chances of success.

It's just as important to keep this realistic attitude when you have achieved success. It will prevent you from either becoming complacent or convinced of your own invincibility, both of which are summed up by the old saying 'Pride comes before a fall'.

50 GOING BEYOND

*Man cannot discover new oceans unless he has the courage
to lose sight of the shore.*
André Gide

*Nothing is so dangerous to the progress of the human mind
than to assume that our views of science are ultimate, that
there are no mysteries in nature, that our triumphs are
complete and that there are no new worlds to conquer.*
Humphry Davy

*For good ideas and true innovation, you need human
interaction, conflict, argument, debate.*
Margaret Heffernan

Innovation is creativity with a job to do.
John Emmerling

*But innovation comes from people meeting up in the hallways
or calling each other at 10:30 at night with a new idea, or
because they realized something that shoots holes in how
we've been thinking about a problem.*
Steve Jobs

This book is only an introduction to the subject of productivity.
As a productive person you can advance well beyond what is in
it. If you have read what is in the book, done the exercises and
are beginning to put the principles into practice, then you are
well on the way to being a productive person. And as such, you
can answer your own questions and find your own methods,
which may be unique to yourself.

Something you can do which is really constructive is to re-read
some of the chapters in the book and make each chapter the
subject of the questioning techniques. Your aim is to go beyond
what is in the chapter for your own particular circumstances.

1 TAKE THE PRINCIPLES IN THIS BOOK AND RUN WITH THEM

This book points you in the right direction, but only you can actually follow the path forwards.

If you are serious about doing this, then the first step is to spend the necessary time to get good low-level routines established. I have mentioned your time management method as being the most essential of these routines. The time management method I described in Chapter 9 is designed for maximum productivity. If you use it consistently you should find that your focus will narrow onto what is essential at the moment. The result will be that you will push your projects to completion instead of leaving them hanging.

Once you've established this and other low-level routines to the level at which you don't need to think about them, you will be in a better position to develop your own higher-level routines.

2 ONCE YOU HAVE GOT THE PRINCIPLES ESTABLISHED IN YOUR LIFE, GO BEYOND THEM

So you've got your time management system working and all the other low level routines in place. You have developed processes for all your current projects. Where to now?

Well, that's exactly the question you should be asking yourself: 'Where to now?' It's at this stage that your own creativity can kick in and take you forward into areas which maybe you haven't considered up to now.

Develop the principles further – you don't need me to do that. You're a productive person now. And as I mentioned earlier, ask questions about each chapter to see how you can expand its contents for your own purposes. Start with the chapters that particularly resonate with you.

3 KEEP PROGRESSING

To be productive you need to continue progressing and developing. You will make mistakes, but remember that a mistake is a chance to learn (see Chapter 11). Learn from your mistakes, and don't give up. The key quality to develop is to be persistent because almost any worthwhile accomplishment needs persistence – persistence in giving the project sufficient regular focused attention.

That persistence in giving projects regular focused attention comes from establishing good routines and processes. A routine is a well-designed routine when it is easier to keep to it than not to keep to it. In other words it has been designed so that it is the path of least resistance for you (see Chapter 4).

Putting it all together

What you should have gathered from this book is that productivity is not something you are born with, but is a learned activity. Like all learned activities it requires practice. But the great thing about it is that anyone can learn to be productive if they are prepared to take the trouble to learn and practise it.

You will not become productive if you just read a few chapters in this or any other book and then do nothing about it. You need to exercise yourself in productivity as seriously as a concert violinist practices the violin. In fact you will be practising even longer hours because you will be using it during your entire work day, and quite possibly during your personal and leisure time as well.

INDEX